1.50

# HOW TO READ HOW-TO
# AND SELF-HELP BOOKS

How to Read How-To and Self-Help Books: Getting Real Results from the Advice You Get.
Copyright © Janne Ruokonen 2003. Janne Ruokonen asserts the moral right to be identified
as the author of this work.

Published 2003 by Rivion Publishing Ltd, London.
Distributed in the US by Rivion North America.

Visit us at www.rivionpublishing.com  and  www.howtoselfhelp.com
Rivion Publishing Ltd, 90-100 Sydney Street, London, SW3 6NJ
e-mail for orders, customer service and permissions publisher@rivionpublishing.com

British Library Cataloguing in Publication Data. A catalogue
record for this book is available from the British Library.

ISBN 0-9543506-0-X

Printed in Germany

Book design by Boris Budeck and Volker Fiedler

The Reader's Responsibility When Using This Book
The author and publisher have done their best to ensure that the information in this book is
correct. This book is intended to provide the reader with general information regarding the
presented subject matter: how to get the most out of using how-to/self-help advice. The reader
should not consider this book a replacement for any form of professional advice which may
be applicable to his or her specific situation or circumstances. The reader is solely responsible
for the use of information in this book. The author or publisher is not responsible for the
reader or for anyone else on account of the information or the lack thereof in this book.

Attention corporations, organizations and educational institutions: This book is available at
special quantity discounts for bulk purchase for promotions, gift-giving, educational purposes, and fund raising. Special books, booklets or book excerpts can also be created to fit specific needs. For information, please contact publisher@rivionpublishing.com.

# HOW TO READ HOW-TO AND SELF-HELP BOOKS:
## Getting Real Results from the Advice You Get

**Janne Ruokonen**

Rivion Publishing

# Contents

# Contents

# Introduction

When was the last time you picked up a self-help or how-to book with the conviction that this time you are *really* going to make that big change in your life or finally learn what you have always wanted to learn? Yet after reading a few chapters you found that the whole thing just sort of slipped through your fingers, your best intentions somehow forgotten, and you never actually got around to doing what you were so enthusiastic about in the first place.

Or, have you ever gone to a motivational seminar and come out really fired up about all the great things that you have the potential to do, only to realize a few weeks later that you've gone back to your old habits?

Or perhaps you have spent a great deal of money on a set of audiotapes which promise to make you successful, help you to lose weight or create the perfect relationship, only to discover that no matter how much you listen to the advice, nothing ever seems to happen.

The fact is, despite the disappointments you may have experienced before, good self-help and how-to advice really *does* work. This book will show you the most effective ways to use personal development books, tapes and seminars in order to get whatever it is you want out of life.

The whole self-help/how-to and motivational industry has been built on the promise of teaching you practical ways of getting what you want. The principle is simple: The key to success is to follow the advice of people who have gone through similar situations or who have had similar experiences. By leveraging their expert knowledge and learning from their successes and failures you can get the results you want. There are more resources than ever in human history to teach you what you need to learn and to help you become what you want to become.

Unfortunately, that's not enough.

The problem with many otherwise excellent self-help and how-to books is that although they contain a great deal of advice, most of them come without instructions on how to put this advice to use to achieve maximum results. Knowing something, without possessing the necessary strategies to turn this knowledge into meaningful action, is not going to help you. In a sense, how-to comes without a "how to." The field of self-development is lacking in essential material which can help you to get the most out of it. No wonder you became frustrated after a few failed attempts!

It is also difficult to know whose advice to follow. There are thousands of how-to and self-help books, audiotapes, videos and seminars available. How do you know which one to choose? How do you know who is giving sound advice and who is just trying to rip you off?

It is not your fault that you failed before. You will get the results that you are looking for when you know how to use the self-help and how-to advice correctly. In this book you will learn how to select the right resources and how to make them work. You will also learn how to get guaranteed results and how to avoid the most common pitfalls which could ruin the whole effort.

This book is not another self-help book offering a step-by-step plan. You will not learn how to become successful by reading this book alone; rather you will learn something more important: how to find and use the best resources available on whatever you want to achieve or become, and how to get real results out of them every time.

Here is my story: During my high school years I stumbled across some self-help books at the local library and immediately became interested in them. One of the first how-to books I read was written by Harvey Mackay, and the title was very intriguing: *Swim With the Sharks Without Being Eaten Alive*. As I was considering going to business school after graduation, Mackay's book on the secrets of success in business was something that I just could not let pass by. After finishing the book, my head was spinning and I thought, "Wow! Someone is giving me advice that has taken years to accumulate, in an area which I know nothing about, and I'm getting it all for the price of a book!" I was simply amazed at what I could learn. What Mackay had to say was so different from what we were taught at school. So, I rushed to the bookstore to buy myself a copy of the book and to see if there were similar books available. What I found was Mark McCormack's *What They Don't Teach You at Harvard Business School*, another classic on how to succeed in the world of business. So, of course, I bought this book as well and both remaining copies of Mackay's book – the one that I had just read at the library – because I didn't want to let anyone else in on the secret. Now there was no turning back – I was hooked on self-help and how-to books.

At some point, however, I discovered that for all the advice provided in the books, I was seeing relatively few results. In spite of believing in what the authors had written, despite the exercises and checklists, somehow the great things promised never quite materialized in my life. As I began wondering why this was so, I somehow instinctively knew that the problem did not lie in the content of the books (since all the advice made sense), and the problem didn't really have to do with me (since I considered myself to be both smart and hardworking) – somehow I had just not found the right strategies to make it all work for me.

However, I kept at it over the years, trying to differentiate between what really works and what doesn't, and I kept trying to understand how to use these books, tapes and seminars in order to get the best possible results. For a short time I even worked at a company that published self-help books and produced motivational seminars. Later, when I began to work in managerial positions for other companies, I always tried to experiment with what I had learned. I attended seminars, interviewed people and researched on-line discussion groups. I started a library containing hundreds of self-help and how-to books, and always took notes on what works and why. As a result, certain patterns began to emerge: there is a practical way to get maximum results out of self-help and how-to books, and these principles can be learned by anyone – saving years of wasted effort and frustration.

This book is about getting real results from the advice you get. Ultimately, I wrote this book because throughout the years of reading self-help and how-to books, this is the one book that I wish I had had when I first began.

# Finding Your Way Around the Book

Depending on your interests, you will find some sections of the book more useful than others. Feel free to skip certain chapters and jump to a topic that interests you more.

This book will guide you through the personal development/ motivational/success category of how-to and self-help advice. It won't offer a unique "success system" in itself. It is meant to be read together with other books that cover the topic you want to learn more about. For example, if you want to learn sales skills, read a how-to book on sales in conjunction with this book.

Here is how the book is organized: PART ONE of the book describes what you can achieve by using self-help and how-to books, tapes and seminars. You will learn who the personal development authors and speakers are and what types of books are available.

PART TWO of the book helps you to understand why you may have failed before, how to avoid the usual pitfalls and how to deal with the paradoxes and contradictions that may confuse you. It will reveal why people become stagnant in their progress and offer ways to overcome these obstacles.

PART THREE of the book will help you to put self-help advice into practice. Following this advice will give you the tools to make a truly lasting change in your life.

If you are looking for self-help/how-to resources to use, the appendix lists a collection of books and other resource material that you can use to expand your knowledge.

# PART ONE

# WHAT YOU CAN ACHIEVE AND WHOSE ADVICE TO FOLLOW

# 1.

# Why Read How-To and Self-Help Books

When you know what to do, how to do it and how to motivate yourself to take action on a regular basis, you can achieve almost anything you have ever dreamed of. You can become successful at anything you desire, whether it be personal growth, better relationships, success at work or how to overcome a particular obstacle. Your future is only limited by your knowledge and by the application of that knowledge to your life. With the right methods and the right amount of effort in putting these methods to work, you can create the kind of life you want.

By reading how-to and self-help books you will benefit from other people's advice, experiences and collective wisdom. You do not have to spend years of trial and error to find out what works. Others have been through it before you, and almost any skill, type of knowledge or habit that you can imagine can be learned. Whatever anybody else has achieved, you can achieve, too, by following in their footsteps.

True, there always seems to be those lucky few who appear to get everything they want without seeming to put forth any effort. While this may look great on the surface, it can be a recipe for disaster when their luck runs out. It is better to know that you have the ablility to create your own luck and that you can get what you want by knowing what to do and how to do it. There will still be times when things do not work out the way you'd like, but when you know how to create your own luck, you will eventually succeed.

How-to and self-help books, tapes and seminars offer practical methods of acquiring new knowledge, skills, habits and ways to personal growth. Throughout this book you will learn how to put this advice into action which will produce results every time.

## Life Is a Do-It-Yourself Project

In many ways life itself is really a self-help, do-it-yourself project. Everyone lives their life the best they can; sometimes life comes with instructions, but more often than not we seem to be missing those few critical pieces of the puzzle which would help us to put it all together.

You go about this project by yourself and therefore whatever you do to make it work could be called self-help or self-improvement. And this is really the only way to develop since nobody else but you can fulfill your potential. For all the advice we receive from the outside, nobody else can live your life for you.

Unfortunately, in an age where we can seek the advice of experts in every possible subject matter in the world, we have come to rely on them to validate our progress or development.

This makes the word self-help sound a bit "unprofessional." Some of us may even feel a little ashamed when we read a how-to book or listen to a set of self-improvement tapes in our car simply because we have gotten used to the idea that learning is supposed to take place in schools, universities or at least under the close guidance of an accredited professional.

But when you see life the way it really is – your biggest do-it-yourself project – you also see that you need to be active in creating the kind of outcome you want. No one will put as much time and effort into your project as you will. No expert will be able to understand your goals or projects more intimately than you can. It is only natural that you want to learn the best way to proceed and pick up a little practical advice to help you along the way.

## Seven Reasons Why Self-Help and How-to Advice Really Works

We've been told that self-help and how-to advice really works if you believe it will work. Here are seven convincing reasons why you should believe this:

### *You create your own world*

The reasons for the present situation in your life come mostly from inside, not outside. You determine what you are and what you do. This is what makes the how-to and self-help books so powerful.

### *You are doing something for yourself*

You have your own personal reasons for working towards your goals, you are motivated and it is for your own benefit.

An outside expert may take a professional interest in helping you, but this is never going to be as strong as your own interest in helping yourself.

### You are truly in control

There will always be some circumstances that are beyond your control, but in the end you are always in charge of your own life. Determine what you want and the how-to advice will present practical ways of achieving this.

### People can help themselves

We all have skills we can use, as we have been able to solve our problems before. Sometimes it only takes a little support from outside – from books, tapes, seminars, friends – to get ourselves to make a successful change inside. By no means does this support always have to be commercial. Think of neighbor-hood clubs and free Internet communities as an example.

### You naturally want to grow

Our need for personal growth is part of our human nature. We all want to improve and evolve in our lives. The important thing is that this motivation for growth comes from the inside rather than being a reaction to outside demands.

### Practical, step-by-step advice gets you started

Most people are not interested in abstract theories. They want to know what works in everyday life, what to focus on, what pitfalls to avoid and what the little tricks are that can only be learned through experience. Practical advice gives you a jump-start and whets your appetite for more.

*The truth is out there*

Any skill – from gardening to parenting to race-car driving, to sales success to jungle survival – has dozens, often hundreds of books, videos, audiotapes and workshops published on the topic. You can find out how to do absolutely anything.

## Are You Working Hard or Working Smart?

Working hard has long been the way success is achieved in our society. However, increasing competition has meant that the forty-hour workweek is not enough anymore. People have responded by working a bit longer every day and putting in a few Saturdays and even Sundays. And for the moment they might be getting ahead of the pack. Unfortunately, *everybody* seems to be putting in more hours at work in order to be more competitive. As a result many of us are still at the same place where we left off, except now we are regularly working 60 hour weeks.

Working hard at our jobs no longer guarantees that we will be successful. In many cases, it does not even bring financial rewards. Instead, many people are more or less just making ends meet by working this hard.

To be successful today, you must do two things. First, you must not only work hard at your job, you must also work hard on yourself. You must put hours into your self-development and into acquiring new knowledge and skills. Second, you must work smart, not just hard. These are the things that you learn from how-to and self-help books, tapes, videos and seminars. When you are working on your own personal development and getting smart about producing results, work becomes more enjoyable and this increases your motivation to do more. When you get smart, it is also easier to keep working hard when you need to.

## Self-Help and How-To Complement Each Other

Although slightly different in orientation, self-help and how-to books work well together, and these two words will be used more or less interchangeably in this book. Both genres are very practical-oriented. The books are written in a style that makes new concepts easy to understand and act upon. Usually the underlying theories or scientific studies are left out in order to concentrate on the heart of the matter – how to quickly improve your present situation.

*How-to* mainly teaches new knowledge and skills, often including tips and hints that come from other people's many and varied experiences in a chosen field. It may touch upon areas such as attitude and motivation but does usually not go very deep. *Self-help,* on the other hand, tends to focus more on the development of overall human potential, covering areas such as beliefs, goal setting, learning new habits and making an overall positive change. It suggests that the ability to achieve anything in your life is controlled by your mental attitude – for example, by the ideas and attitudes you adopt.

Consider a person who wants to become a top salesperson in his or her field. A how-to book on sales strategies would be an obvious place to start. It would describe the ways other people have achieved sales success and perhaps it would offer a program to follow. However, this advice would be even more useful if this individual also found a book or a seminar on self-motivation and attitude. After all, sales strategies will be of little use if the motivation and the right kind of attitude to implement them is lacking. Combined, how-to and self-help offer a strong basis for improving your life.

## Why Your Present Skills and Knowledge
## Are Not Enough

Your present skills and abilities got you where you are today. If you want to improve your life, you must improve your abilities. And you must improve them on two accounts. First, you need to upgrade your knowledge. Second, you need to turn your knowledge into intelligent action.

Your knowledge starts becoming outdated the moment you take it in. Consider this example: how much is the knowledge of the 1995 computer technology, however detailed, worth now? Although it represented the absolute cutting edge in its time, now it is worth next to nothing. What is really striking is that even when you do not work in this particular industry, any changes still have an enormous impact on you. The same goes for medicine, communications or commerce. Even if you are at the top of your field, unless you continuously update your knowledge and skills, you stand to lose out to those who learn more and update their knowledge faster.

Even knowledge itself will no longer provide you with a competitive edge – only learning new skills and applying this knowledge will. The skills and habits that you have today will not be sufficient tomorrow. Whether you like it or not, you must constantly learn new habits and skills and update the old. You simply have no choice. Learning how to develop these new abilities is perhaps the most important investment you can make in your life. How-to and self-help resources can help you to get organized and to take practical steps by bringing a little structure and action orientation into your learning.

## Reality Check: You Can Have Anything
## But Not Everything

While you can learn anything you set your mind to and become virtually anything you desire, there are still very real limitations in each of our lives that make certain goals particularly hard to reach. It has not exactly done wonders to the credibility of how-to and self-help advice that the most often repeated phrase is "you can do anything."

You can have almost anything but you cannot have everything. Having everything you can imagine is just not possible. Rest assured that your imagination can work faster and stretch further than your ability to ever make it real. Do not fool yourself. Think about what you really want to have and what you really need to have – then use self-help and how-to advice to help you achieve these goals. However, if you imagine having anything and everything that pops into your head, set that as your goal and try to achieve it by attending a few motivational seminars that promise you the world, and you're bound to be disappointed!

Some things are reachable only by discarding everything else in your life. They take up so much time and effort that you have very little time and energy left for anything else. If this is what you are willing to do, fine. But when you discover that you have to sacrifice everything to achieve one single goal, you might decide that it is not really worth it. The cost is simply too high. This is the very real meaning of the saying, "You can have anything you want just as long as you want it badly enough and are willing to make the sacrifices to get it." Not all sacrifices are worth making, even if it is possible for you to make them.

There are also some things that you cannot change. You can

only learn to live with these things by changing your attitude and what they mean to you. A healthy dose of realism is to recognize that while it is true that you can have virtually anything you want, it is also true that you cannot have everything. Human life has limitations. By understanding these boundaries, you will get more out of how-to and self-help than if you believe that everything is magically going to come true in your life.

## What You Will Gain

You will receive a wide range of benefits from using self-help and how-to advice which will help to improve your and other people's lives:

### *Learn from other people's experience*

Learning only from your own personal experience is slow and prone to errors. There simply isn't enough time to do it all yourself. You can skip years of wasted effort by finding out what other people have done before you and by applying their wisdom to your life.

### *Get an edge*

You can get advice from the best in the business, often for the price of a book or even at no cost at all. You can find out what makes the small but decisive difference between doing something well and doing it superbly and you can learn the tricks of the trade directly from world-class experts.

### *Take some time for yourself*

Self-help and how-to allow you to think about yourself: Who you are, what you do, what you want, what motivates you, what you believe in, how you behave and how you feel. Give yourself time to find the answers to the important questions in your life.

*Gain support and motivation*

You will not feel alone or odd when you discover that others have been down the same road before you, others have had their questions answered, and others have found out what works. Human challenges and solutions are universal.

# A Word for Skeptics:
# The Most Common Misconceptions
# about Self-Help

Everybody has an opinion about self-help and how-to advice. For some, it is a great tool, and for others it is something they would never even consider. There are also people who are prejudiced against the whole idea that you could proactively change yourself for the better or that such a change could ever last. Even those people who actively read how-to books and attend training workshops themselves may harbor some mental objections or unclear questions regarding self-help and how-to advice.

Not everything that is said or written in the field of self-development is correct. As in every area of commercial life, everything is available – from truly bad advice to top-of-the-range advice, and everything in between. You have to know how to differentiate between the real thing and the bogus, and you are right to be skeptical if something sounds too good to be true. However, there is probably more lost human potential than we can imagine because many people have mistaken impressions and negative attitudes towards the whole field of self-improvement. It is time to dispel these myths. Here are the most common self-help and how-to misconceptions and the reasons not to believe them:

## Misconception: It Will Turn You into Another Person

*"Self-help just tries to make us into something we are not. Why can't we just be satisfied with being who we are?"*

People are "works in progress." You are not static, you evolve. You have a natural craving to try new things, to develop your abilities and to be good at something. Wanting to be more than you are now, or just wanting things to be different, is perfectly normal. Even if you are not interested in self-development for yourself, maybe there are people around you whose lives you would like to make richer and happier. As you do things for others, you often come to realize that some aspects of your own personality are evolving as well.

Most people just want to improve certain aspects of their lives, not change everything or become another person. No matter how much you work on yourself, you suddenly cannot become someone else or turn into a stranger to all the people around you. Your experiences, relationships and the society you live in have shaped you into what you are today. You can only develop this person more intensively. And, if you are happy with everything and feel that there is no need to change – great, enjoy it!

## Misconception: Smart People Don't Need Self-Help Advice

*"I am too intelligent and educated to believe in self-help. It is not meant for me."*

It may be precisely your intellect that prevents you from acting upon simple advice and thus keeps you from reaching your full potential. For highly-intelligent people, the success steps featured in self-help books and workshops may seem too easy and simple. If you belong to this school of thought, you rationalize that if success were that easy, then everybody would be successful, and since this is not the case, these books must be a sham.

You want something new and more sophisticated, and refuse to consider self-help because you don't want to admit that the real world is full of simple, even mundane repetitive tasks that just have to be done if you want to achieve something. Just because the steps are simple does not mean that they cannot lead you to success. They may be simple yet surprisingly hard to carry out. Every smoker knows that smoking is bad for their health, yet they find it surprisingly difficult to stop. Every child knows that if they concentrate on their homework, they will do better at school, yet many find themselves completely unmotivated by their books. And everybody knows that if they get into better shape the quality of their life will improve, yet most people still fail to do it.

If you believe that you can't benefit from self-help and how-to advice, you are probably too smart for your own good. You are both blessed and cursed with your above-average intelligence. This can make it harder for you to achieve true success than for others who are more open to the idea. Your intellect has probably already helped you to achieve much in your life and perhaps has made you feel a bit superior, making it that much harder to let go of your old attitudes and habits.

Don't fall into the intelligence trap. Listen to the successful business managers or sports coaches talk about the reasons behind their success. Invariably, they say that they work hard at getting the basics down. You don't need any magic formulas or rocket science to improve your life, but you do need a healthy dose of humility in order not to shun ideas just because they are "simple."

*"I have read a few of these books and they all follow the same basic pattern. I could easily do it all if I just wanted to."*

You might think that you already know all there is to know about what's written in self-help books. You might also think that there is nothing new you could learn from them and that you don't need motivation. And since you already "know" the main principles, you think you could get down to business just by putting your mind to it. In reality, you are fooling yourself.

What is happening here is that you are not doing anything, you are just *thinking* about doing something – and that alone will not get you anywhere. You may actually be taking yourself further and further away from achieving your goals because thinking, analyzing and treating everything as an intellectual exercise may even prevent you from actually getting out of your chair and doing something.

Because you are intelligent, you are capable of coming up with rationalizations in order to justify your actions. You want to remain within the realm of your intellect, taking great pride in your ability to think complex thoughts. You want to do everything with your head instead of involving your heart, your feelings and your gut reactions. But you may have simply lost touch with the real world where something great is achieved daily by repeating the same simple tasks over and over again.

*"I already know everything there is to know about how to improve. I don't need to pay good money to hear it all again!"*

That is exactly the problem: you just know *about* it. But you have not turned your knowledge into action. There is a world of difference between the two. Remember, you do not get into shape just by knowing all about fitness, you only get into shape by *doing* regular exercise. Knowledge alone will take you nowhere.

When you really internalize something, you turn it into action. If you haven't been able to change your behavior with this knowledge, then you have not really internalized it. (Yes, your behavior could be purely intellectual, but even then it is manifested in concrete actions.) Before thoughts can be transformed into action, you need to hear the same thing over and over again. If the skill or habit you want to acquire is an important one, it might be a good idea to invest some money to hear what the experts have to say until you fully internalize the message.

Ask any self-development coach and they will tell you that the people who buy the most books and attend the most seminars are those who need it the least. The most successful people are not just looking for new knowledge, they are trying to internalize it and turn what they already know into effective action. In order to accomplish this, they keep listening to the same message over and over again until it becomes part of who they are.

Contrary to what many people believe, you often need somebody else to tell you what you already know. It is not stupid to do this; on the contrary, it is actually a very intelligent idea because it reinforces the message and helps you to really internalize the idea.

## Misconception: I Read the Book But It Did Not Work

*"I read the book / went to a seminar / listened to a set of audio
tapes, but it didn't work. Nothing happened."*

A book cannot work for you, only you can make something
work. Nothing will happen just by reading books or attending
seminars. You must make things happen yourself. Nobody else,
no matter how good a writer or a speaker they may be, can do it
for you.

Following other people's advice *does* work – it has worked for
thousands of people, but only if you turn what you have learned
into consistent action.

*"My friend, who had cancer, went through all the self-help
books, New Age healing and spiritual guides but died anyway.
This stuff doesn't work."*

Self-help is not a cure-all or panacea. The truth is, we do not
always get what we want or need in life, no matter how hard we
try. Self-help is also not about replacing science (in this case
medical science) nor is it about working miracles.

Claiming that something does not work because there are
examples of it not working is not very constructive. Very few
things work 100% of the time. We fly in airplanes although we
know that some of them have crashed, we get married although
we know that many couples get divorced. Many people do find
help for their illnesses through self-help although there are also
many whose condition cannot be improved no matter what they
do. Taking action does not guarantee success, but it sure increases
its chances.

*"This book made me think but failed to give practical
and clear solutions."*

Not everything can be solved. There are situations where there are simply very few answers available. Not everything in human life can be managed, handled or neatly organized. We have to face the fact that there are no clear-cut answers or solutions to certain issues. When a loved one dies or someone is born with a serious disability, we feel helpless or even angry because there is so little that we can actually do. Sometimes we can only cope with a situation, perhaps grow to understand it and find consolation in this, but this does not make the situation go away. At best, we can learn to live with these issues and find the courage to look forward despite them.

## Misconception: It Is All Just Common Sense

*"Nothing this simple can be effective. If it were this simple,
everybody would do it."*

First, it sounds simple because often it *is*. Somehow we think that in order for anything to be any good in the modern world, it has to be complex in order to be effective. This is not true. Simple actions, repeated over time, produce the most extraordinary results. Looking for sophistication may lead you to overlook those simple and proven success methods which could also work for you. You need a dose of humility to stick to the basics every day.

Second, as explained earlier in this chapter, simple is by no means always easy to carry out. Not everybody has the motivation and discipline to do even the simplest things.

*"It is all just common sense."*

It is true that much of self-help advice is common sense. If it weren't, most of us would have a difficult time trusting it and learning it quickly. Self-development ideas will not be totally new because they can be related to or linked to something that everybody in the audience already knows. Most of the time human knowledge is refined further on the basis of what already exists; only rarely is there a new idea or a method which has no connection to anything that is already known.

When we can link the message to what we already know, we memorize and process it easily. That is why self-help authors try to make their examples simple and commonplace. Then everybody, even in a large audience, has a reference point which makes the message easy to understand, reinforce and act upon. This is also why some academics, with their own well-developed knowledge structures and scientific expressions, tend to sneer at everything in this field. When all they hear is layman's language, they mistakenly think that the message must be simplistic as well.

The advice appears simple because a great deal of effort has gone into making it easily communicated and understood. Do not mistake the message for something simplistic or easy to carry out. Surprisingly few of us are able to consistently put all that common sense to good use.

*"It is just about positive thinking."*

There is more to it than that. Positive thinking can help you to create a mind-set that is receptive to learning new things, but it alone will not get you very far. Most of the modern self-development coaches believe that you need to see things realistically, and that reality shouldn't be obscured or veiled by overly-positive thinking.

Sometimes it is not the message but rather the coaches and authors themselves whom we find exasperatingly positive. But, would you rather listen to a message from someone whose head is hanging down, who doesn't have any confidence and who is a negative person as well? Speakers have learned that an enthusiastic frame of mind infects them with enegy and makes training more effective. In addition, many authors and trainers feel that they themselves are still learning something new as they teach others, thus making them even more enthusiastic about their message.

### Misconception: It Is Not Scientific

*"There is little scientific basis in self-help."*

Many concepts in how-to and self-help programs have a solid foundation in science. Certainly, they are often popularized versions, but you need a jumping-off place and usually people find it easiest without abstract theories and difficult language to contend with. What people really appreciate in their busy lives is somebody who just gets them started.

There is nothing stopping you from seeking answers for self-development from modern psychology, sociology, cognitive science and philosophy as well, but whether you listen to a scientist or a layman, nothing guarantees that the person is always right. You need to use your own judgment.

*"Self-help offers simplistic advice for complex problems. There is no hard theory to back it up."*

Theories are very useful, but they are only one form of communication and an impressive theory may not always be helpful in real life. When was the last time you heard academics use language that was easily understood, colorful, and included great stories to boot? When was the last time you heard them speak using a language which was passionate, offered encouragement, was convincing and simplified complex terms? When was the last time academic language interacted with you, communicated with your feelings and touched your heart?

Language must be used in a way that will make an impact. Typical scientific language is very precise but so full of reservations and "ifs and buts" that it quickly loses its power. In order to get through to you and encourage you to take action, language must be easily understood and encouraging. It should rely on anecdotes, checklists, aphorisms and analogies in order to have an emotional effect on you. Cold facts or hard theory rarely inspire you. Funnily enough, this is supported by scientific studies which state that the majority of human communication is not contained or transmitted through words themselves but rather by the tone, form and delivery of those words.

The key issue is not whether people can understand things intellectually – they most certainly can – the key issue for most of us is whether we actually do something useful with our knowledge. Many academics possess a great deal of knowledge but fail to embody it in their actions, and therefore also failing to convince or persuade others of the value of their message. But the self-help gurus are often masters at communicating through emotions and connecting certain emotional states with their messages, thus inspiring us to take immediate action.

*"You can learn all you need to know at the university."*
If academic study were all that was required for success, then

most business school students would become millionaires. Yet curiously many of them work their whole lives for other people and are far from rich. Just ask yourself this: Did you learn everything you needed to know about your present job while you were at the university?

*"There are no 'secrets of success.' This is just a rip off."*

Yes, there are scams. The amazing power of magic stones (order now – just $39.95!) will probably not turn you into a mind-reader, although some people will go and swear on TV that they really work. There is, however, no reason to stop driving a car just because you know that there are some dishonest used-car salespeople out there. With a healthy dose of common sense you can usually smell a potential scam miles away.

Magic stones might not cut it, but applying the principles and lessons learned by others will – whether you want to become a better manager, find the relationship you are looking for, or learn how to create a beautiful garden. Since people are naturally intrigued by the new and the unknown, these principles might be called "secrets" or "amazing discoveries." But keep in mind that this is just marketing sizzle to catch your attention – look beyond it to see if there is a steak cooking back there, too.

## Misconception: You Can't Coach Tiger Woods

*"Only beginners need this kind of help. When you already know what you are doing, you don't need to bother with it anymore."*

Tiger Woods is probably the best golf player ever. Could somebody possibly offer him advice on playing better golf? You bet! Tiger Woods is coached on a number of things from proper nutrition to fitness training to developing mental stamina. All of these areas are vital for a top player, and Tiger Woods receives a good deal of advice on how to master them. Not only that, there are still areas of the game itself where some players are still better than he is, but Tiger is catching up. The best of the bunch are always looking to learn more.

Perhaps the best word to describe what Tiger Woods is receiving is "facilitation." He uses others to support and help him, but in the end he is the one who must be responsible for the actual learning and putting the final package together. This is how it is in every other area of life as well. So, when you become very, very accomplished in your chosen field and believe that nobody could possibly teach you anything of value, think about Tiger Woods and all the hours he still spends getting coached – and get back to work.

*"Compared to others, I'm already successful. I don't need to bother with self-development."*

If you're only interested in self-improvement just to make yourself better than others, you will quickly come up against a brick wall. Judge yourself according to your own potential, and don't only strive to improve yourself, but also strive to make other people's lives better.

Tiger Woods doesn't play golf only with the intention of defeating other players; he has already done that. He plays to beat his own record. He plays to be the best he can be. And that is why he is as good as he is.

# Choosing the Right Advice

There are currently more than 80,000 book titles published every year in the US alone. There are thousands of self-help books available with hundreds more being added every year. In addition, there are thousands of audio tapes, videos, live seminars, workshops, magazines on specific topics, Internet resources and user groups trying to catch your attention – not to mention the resources which are available internationally.

How can you choose the best advice for you? Of course, it depends on what you want, but there is more to it than that. You need to know what kind of help will get you started and what will help to keep you going. You need to know who the authors and speakers are and what kind of approaches they take. You need to know how and why you should combine different resources to get the best results. Before selecting the type of advice you need, you should also understand the reasons why almost everything works.

## The Dirty Little Secret: Everything Works...

Many social, organizational and psychological studies have shown that most of the methods used to improve a situation, whether in a work setting or in private life, actually do work. Surprisingly, whatever you do, works. How can this be?

The unsettling fact is that almost anything works because usually just by intervening in the current situation, you'll get some results. Simply by breaking your previous thought patterns and your former way of doing things, you already change something and open the door to improvement. When you interrupt the status quo, no matter what method you use, you become aware of what is happening and start paying conscious attention to what you are doing and why you are doing it. This is something that you may not normally do in day-to-day life, where you most likely find yourself jumping from one busy task to another on autopilot.

There is a famous study which was conducted in the thirties called the Hawthorne Study, in which the relationship between the working conditions in a factory and the produced output was studied. The study involved measuring the output under normal conditions and then comparing the results to the outcome when working conditions were improved. Sure enough, when more light was added, productivity went up, and when short breaks were added every few hours, productivity increased again. So, researchers were about to conclude that improving working conditions increased productivity, until they decided to verify their findings by returning conditions to the way they used to be (logically, productivity should then go down). But something very surprising happened: contrary to their expectations, productivity stayed up! The researchers were dumbfounded, how could this be? Slowly, the answer emerged. The workers did not become more productive because of the improved conditions, but rather because for the first time someone was paying attention to what they were doing.

This is why it does not always matter very much which how-to book you pick up or which self-improvement seminar you attend. Just the fact that you are paying attention to yourself and to your behavior will produce results. This is true especially in the beginning, where just about anything you do to break your current pattern will work. Therefore, it is often much more important for you just to get started than to try to look for the perfect workshop or book.

## ...For a While

Even imperfect self-improvement and how-to advice works because it helps to focus your attention on what you are doing. Although everything seems to work for a while, often the changes tend not to last very long.

What may have worked initially as a kind of "shock-therapy" soon begins to wear off. You will revert to your old ways once the first rush wears off and you don't know how to keep it up day after day. The output on the factory floor will return to normal after the researchers have left and nobody is there to pay attention to the workers anymore.

You may also find that there is the so-called "placebo effect" at work. This comes from the field of medical research where one test group is given the actual drug and the control group is given a placebo. Both groups are told that the pills will improve their health. Invariably, one-fifth of the placebo group reports the same results as the control group, showing improvement in their condition, simply because they believe that they have been given the real drug. Self-development trainers have used this fact as an example to demonstrate the tremendous power of our beliefs. But there is another lesson to be learned as well: everything may work for a while, just because we think it will. There is always going to be a group of people who seems to get results using the most exotic methods imaginable (think of examples such as Origami or mud-wrestling used as relationship therapy). However, if there is no real benefit behind the method, most of us will show no improvement and even many of those who do later end up back where they started.

Check whether the method you want to try is logical – it is preferable if there is some research to back it up. There is no guarantee that it will work for you or that it will bring long-term results just because it worked for someone else. It can be fun trying something totally different which sparks your interest. Often new innovations originate from outside of traditional methods. Remember, however, that something usually enters the mainstream for the reason that it works for the majority of people.

How can you make an improvement last then? To achieve a lasting impact, new *habits* need to be created. When an action becomes a habit, you are no longer aware of the single actions which must be consciously taken every time because the desired actions come more or less automatically. This will be explored in detail in the third part of this book.

## Three Ways to Choose

How should you choose between all the different books, tapes and workshops? There are three ways to get started:

*Take Fast Action*

The solution lies in the field of self-help and how-to itself. These books (or tapes) are written to be used, not just to be read! Their practical orientation encourages you to take action. So, take action! Take the first book within your reach which seems to make sense, and then begin. Skip the arduous process of selection altogether. Just go to the bookstore and pick a book which seems to make sense. Then go home and start reading.

You have just accomplished two things. You now have a book or a tape that you can use and you have already conditioned yourself to take action – the key quality you must have if you are to get anything out of your selected resource. You can always go back and do some additional research when you select your next book. Moreover, you will then have the advantage of having gone through one book already, knowing a bit better what you would like to find the next time.

*Go Back to What You Have*

If you already have some self-help or how-to books, decide that they will do for the time being. There is a reason you chose them in the first place, so they must contain something interesting. Use your time to read through the book you're now holding in your hands and then apply what you have learned to the books you already have. The reading experience will be quite different compared to the first time. You can always look for new resources later.

*Research and Select*

If there is a specific topic you want to find out more about, check the bookstore databases, enquire at the public libraries or do a search on the Internet bookstores and free search engines.

If your topic is very specific, your list will be somewhat short as there may only be a limited amount of information available. As a result, selecting a book that you can begin with should be fairly easy. You can supplement this by finding resources in areas which support your main interest (use the resource list at the end of this book).

If your topic is generic, such as how to achieve sales success, you can use the following list to narrow down your search: Find out who the prominent authors in the field are; find out who has a name in the industry; find out who is new and who has been around for decades; find out which work is considered classic; find out who speaks the same kind of language as you do; find out who has produced a series of books or tapes; and finally, find out what your friends have tried and what they can recommend.

Just start somewhere and expand to other resources as your knowledge grows. Don't try to find "the best book" – it doesn't exist. Expand your tastes and preferences gradually and you will then discover that you automatically know after a quick glance whether or not a certain book or tape is relevant to you.

## The Concept of Value:
## How Much is Good Advice Really Worth?

If self-improvement is an investment in yourself, just how much should you be willing to invest and what kind of return can you expect? In order to know what to spend your time and money on, you need to understand why things are of very different value to different people.

If you are wondering whether or not it is worth buying a $19.95 self-improvement book, there are two different answers to this question. First of all, of course it is! Twenty dollars is nothing if even one single thing in your life changes for the better as a result of reading that book. You have spent twenty dollars on less valuable things in the past. Secondly, if you are still wondering whether the book is worth it, then maybe it isn't. Perhaps you somehow sense that you would just read a few chapters but take no real action to change anything and the money would thus be completely wasted. Then you are right again – don't buy the book.

Incidentally, the same book or workshop can be worth ten times the cover price to somebody and not worth a dime to somebody else. *You* decide what you are going to get out of it. In addition, people who have already made a positive change in their lives seem to get the most out of reading even more about the topic. They can see how they will put to use what they read, they can see how it will support and help them, and they can see that this is time and money well spent. They will not hesitate to spend a hundred dollars on a set of tapes; they know that they will get their money's worth. This will not happen because the set of tapes is larger than life, but because they put the contents of the tapes to work for themselves.

Value is not something that is objective and independent of you. Things have value to you only because you assign them value. Particularly in the area of how-to and self-help advice, what you get out of this advice depends on how much you are willing to work to extract the value. You can buy all the books in the world, but they aren't going to do you any good if you don't put the ideas to use as well.

The following example is not entirely fair to those people who put a great deal of effort into creating good books or tapes, but it serves to illustrate a point. The reason that a set of self-help audio tapes on "Quitting Smoking in 10 Steps" costs $49.95 is because it happens to be the price the audiotape market can bear. When you think about it, a person who is trying to quit smoking would easily pay ten times as much to succeed. The cost would be recovered in under a year, not to mention what would be gained in terms of health benefits. But here is the catch: The set of audiotapes is priced at $49.95 because it is not really worth anything more. It is not the actual audiotapes that make people stop smoking; the people themselves must do it with the information contained on the tapes. That is where the most value is. The value is not really in *knowing how* you could stop smoking, it lies in *actually doing it.*

This is one of the reasons workshops and seminars are more expensive than books and tapes. Yes, the seminar market generally has always had a higher price range, but what actually justifies that higher price? It is justified if during the seminar the trainer can somehow encourage you to take action which brings you closer to your goals – often you can take the first steps during the very seminar you are attending. When that happens, there is clearly more value than if the knowledge had been transferred via a book or audiotape and you ended up with information instead of concrete action.

Taken to its logical conclusion, one-on-one coaching is the most expensive form of advice because it's also the most valuable. You are getting coached and pushed to act on a regular basis, which is one of the most effective ways towards personal improvement. However, famous trainers can earn more by holding a seminar for 500 attendees than by working with single clients, so not all offer private coaching anymore.

So, the next time you are considering whether to spend money on something that promises to bring you closer to your goals, remember that you get what you pay for. But money is only one aspect of what you need to pay – the results come only when you are willing to spend time and put in the required effort as well.

### Are You Looking to Learn Skills or Attitudes?

Depending on what you want to learn, you need to find different resources and adopt different strategies. When you want to acquire specific knowledge or learn a specific skill, you need to find an expert in the given field. There is usually going to be more than one, so at least initially you need to make a choice between them. Remember that it is more important to get started than to look for the perfect solution. For the best results, integrate the resources on specific skills with those which focus on improving your motivation and beliefs. This will help you learn faster and turn your new skills into habits of a lifetime.

When you are looking to acquire a new habit or work on your motivational level, there are always several places to start. Many of the abilities you want to develop fall under the overlapping categories of cognitive or thinking-skills, life-management, self-motivation and achievement. The "success principles" tend to be generic and there are hundreds of authors proposing essentially the same methods. Whether you start from the viewpoint of business success, personal achievement or the improvement of any human condition, you usually end up heading in the same direction. Things like commitment, strongly believing in yourself, clear goals, planning, communication, teamwork and patience usually come through as the bare essentials required for any achievement. Therefore, personal preferences of style and context set aside, almost any book, tape or a workshop is a good place to start.

There is no need to look for the absolute latest book on the market since most of the ideas have already been well established for a long time. In fact, many of the bestselling books or tapes on the market may be a decade or two old, proof that their message is still relevant today. The seminar market tends to move a little faster, and although the titles of the proffered programs will change, the basic contents largely stay the same. To find out what is available, read the next chapter on authors and speakers, and check the resource list at the end of this book.

## Why No Single Book Has All the Answers

One book or workshop rarely gives you everything you need. To get a broader view, you need to go to other books to find new ideas or to uncover different angles of the same issue.

A book must focus on only one given subject, and a seminar can only run for a certain length of time, which means that much information has to be excluded. Also, if you want to get the message across to as many people as possible, it has to be done with relatively simple language. The examples you use have to be such that you can find common ground among the vast majority of readers. In the process some nuances might be lost. Complex issues often have to be simplified to the point where they no longer do justice to the many sides of the issue which are involved.

If you were pressed for time, couldn't you simply pick the most famous title from your chosen area and just read that one book? Yes, this would certainly be a good way to start, but at some point you would find that some of your questions have still gone unanswered. Life is just too variable – your situation and set of circumstances are far too unique for just one person to provide you with all the answers. Besides, the current bestseller might be far from being the best resource on the subject.

The famous *80/20 rule* states that 80% of the results usually come from the 20% of the work. In this case, it means that a single book or course will have a few key points that will benefit you greatly, while most of the material is not likely to make such a difference. In most books, there are a few key points which are then emphasized throughout the book with dozens of examples and case studies. This keeps the book coherent, but does not explore all the possible views on any given subject.

Rest assured that all the answers you are looking for can be found; sometimes they will just have to be gathered from different sources and applied to your particular situation. No single book or guru will have all the answers. And even if they did, *you* are still the one who needs to process the ideas and give them meaning in your life; that is, making it all relevant to your unique situation.

## The Feel Good Resources

There are a number of books in the self-help category which are essentially feel-good products. They contain mostly stories, quotes and anecdotes that aim to make you feel good about yourself. There is nothing wrong with this – we all need some encouragement, understanding and reassurance that we are OK. We are surrounded by so much negative news and so many adverse events that some time spent with human faith, courage and compassion can only do us good.

This type of book should not become a way to escape reality, however. Feeling good about yourself is great, but you don't want to feel so good about everything that you no longer feel any need to take action to improve what actually needs to be improved. The story of the young boys who pulled a drowning man out of a river using teamwork and courage is heartwarming. But if the only practical advice you get out of this account is that you should believe in teamwork and be courageous, you will not have the right tools in your toolbox in order to know how to put these concepts into practice. The story has served as a reminder of the things you already knew, and although this is valuable in itself, it has not shown you how to acquire new skills or habits – which is essential when you truly want to improve your life.

## Beware of the Quick Fix

You do not always want to change your whole life. Many people would be very happy just to find a "quick fix" for a specific issue that is bothering them. Recognizing this, marketers will sell you anything from *Ten Minutes to a Perfect Relationship* to *Fast, Effortless and Permanent Weight Loss While Watching TV* to *Easy Steps to Earning $10,000 a Month at Home, in Your Pajamas, with Your Left Hand, Your Eyes Closed, Whatever You Want to Believe...*

The temptation to try something that promises effortless results is strong. However, you know that for the things you really want in life – the big things – there is no quick fix available. You can only build a successful career or create a loving relationship with a long-term commitment and persistent and regular effort.

Moreover, you can only *continue* to keep something of value if you know how to take care of it. Someone could hand you a top position in a leading company in your field, yet you would not be able to hang on to it for long if you didn't already have what it takes to get there in the first place. Sooner or later someone would find out that you don't really have the skills it takes to do that job well and the free lunch would be over.

Certain self-help books go as far as to claim that no quick fixes exist. This is not exactly true, either. There are quick fixes because there are several routes that you can take to arrive at your goal. However, the quickest route may not always be the smartest or the most sustainable choice. You may be in the habit of yelling at other people when you are angry, for example. There is no denying that this allows you to vent your feelings and quickly achieve your goal of getting rid of your anger. Unfortunately, it is not a smart or a sustainable strategy – you may find that people around you are beginning to avoid you or may even downright refuse to deal with you. Worse, by choosing the strategy of "yelling your anger away," you have done nothing to change the reasons why you became so angry in the first place; you have merely fixed the symptoms. As a result, the problem is likely to return, and you may have even created more problems because of your reaction.

Typical examples of quick fixes are lying to yourself, masking or hiding your feelings, artificially stimulating your system, and abusing other people's time and good faith. A quick fix may sometimes help momentarily, and it is not necessarily dangerous as long as you are aware of its limitations. But usually, a quick fix is unproductive and a waste of your time. It may work a few times, but the effect will soon wear off. You may just fix the symptoms and not cure the real problem. Your system may get used to the quick fix and begin to require more to get the same effect as before. You may also become frustrated because you know you are avoiding the long-term solution by doing something you really shouldn't be doing.

## Jump-Start Your System

When you have found something you would like to try, make it more effective by devoting enough time and intensity to it.

Sometimes a shock to your system is the best way to wake it up. This could include going to an intensive full-day seminar or retreating to a countryside lodge for the weekend with just the book you are planning to read in tow. It could mean a set of audiotapes coupled with headphones and five hours of unbroken time at home (remember to unplug the telephone). Personal development seminars and workshops work particularly well because someone else is in charge of running and organizing the day and you are not as likely to find excuses to cancel if you've already paid for it. Often this jump-start is all you need to get started and commit to making changes in your life.

Listening to a set of tapes for half an hour every day on your way to work or reading a book every now and then is not going to be as effective. Your mind is preoccupied with other things, the time you're spending on it is short and the intensity and concentration is low. On the other hand, a four-day seminar is also not ideal. Because it is so long, it can be too intensive, introducing too many ideas at once and not giving you enough time to digest everything.

Too little or too much intensity does not create enough momentum to get you off the ground. The inertia of your old habits will be too strong, or you will be too exhausted to transform your new ideas into action. A jump-start should energize you to take action, not leave you indifferent or too exhausted.

When you jump-start your system with a full-day's effort, you will feel victorious because you have finally gotten going. This will motivate you to take immediate follow-up action and it will also make you feel that the time you spent was worthwhile.

## Checklist: Choosing the Resources

Use this checklist to remind yourself how to choose among all the  different books, tapes and seminars available on the market. In addition, read the next chapter to discover who the authors and speakers are who are currently creating these materials.

- Everything works, at least initially. The important thing is to start paying attention to what it is exactly that you want to improve.
- Although everything works, there are still real differences between methods. Use your common sense, but be open to discovering new things as well.
- Action produces initial changes, habits produce permanent changes.
- Don't look for the perfect book or  workshop, get started immediately by using what is easily available. In the beginning, the most important thing is simply to begin.
- Use several resources. It will round up your knowledge and increase your understanding by exposing you to different viewpoints.
- Find resources that give you practical tools as well as inspiration.
- Beware of the quick fix. There is no shortcut to the really valuable things in life.

# Who Are the Authors and Speakers?

Who are the people who write how-to books, hold motivational seminars and sell self-improvement audiotapes? How do they know all that stuff? Where do they come from and what drives them to spread their message?

These people can roughly be divided into two groups. The first group consists of those who write because they are very experienced or skilled in (typically) one area. In other words, they are experts on specific subjects. The subjects are as varied as life, ranging from founding a company to fixing old cars to developing better relationships. Many people become experts through years of experience in their chosen professions, be it accounting, sports coaching or marital counseling. People from this group usually keep practicing their original professions, pursuing their second career as authors, speakers or trainers only part time.

The second group consists of those who are in the so-called

self-development or training business. These people offer their advice on a wide range of subjects, typically specializing in several areas. They are the widely-known professional speakers and authors whose full-time business is to provide people with advice on any kind of achievement from sales success to better parenting. They usually have their own company, sell their products and run the speaking circuit. They may do corporate training and consulting as well as publishing newsletters or Web sites. The most popular are featured on audio cassettes, videos and TV.

## Who Are People Reading and Listening to?

It is difficult to say exactly what is self-help and how-to, and what is not. Some people wouldn't like to be associated with those terms at all. For example, many business book authors consider themselves to be consultants and strategists, not personal development coaches. But it is not hard to see that business gurus like Tom Peters, Harvey Mackay, Mark McCormack and many others are indeed offering advice that is very similar to what you would get from the people in the "traditional" self-development field.

Definite lines are hard to draw, but compare the fictitious titles such as *Gardening for Beginners*, which would probably be found on the hobbies shelf, and *Gardening as a Way to Heal Your Soul*, which would get placed in the self-help section. Both are giving gardening related how-to advice and encouraging improvement, but the approach is completely different.

Let's skip the discussion about what belongs to self-improvement and what doesn't and look at some of the bestselling how-to/self-help book titles from over the past ten years (not in ranking order):

- *A Body For Life*, Bill Phillips, Michael D'Orso
- *Who Moved My Cheese*, Spencer Johnson, M.D.
- *Dr. Atkins' New Diet Revolution*, Robert C. Atkins, M.D.
- *What to Expect When You're Expecting*, Arlene Eisenberg, Heidi E. Murkoff, Sandee E. Hathaway
- *The Art of Happiness: A Handbook for Living*, Dalai Lama, Howard C. Cutler, M.D.
- *The Seven Habits of Highly Effective People*, Stephen R. Covey
- *Men Are from Mars, Women Are from Venus*, John Gray
- *One Day My Soul Just Opened Up*, Iyanla Vanzant
- *The 9 Steps to Financial Freedom*, Suze Orman
- *Simple Abundance*, Sarah Ban Breathnach
- *The Zone: A Dietary Road Map to Lose Weight Permanently*, Barry Sears with Bill Lawren
- *The Seven Spiritual Laws of Success*, Deepak Chopra
- *A Return to Love*, Marianne Williamson
- *Wealth Without Risk: How To Develop a Personal Fortune Without Going Out on a Limb*, Charles J. Givens

Notice how different these titles are from each other. Topics dealing with wealth, health and happiness are always on top of the list, but any one of them might have the makings of this year's bestseller. When you are looking for inspiration, don't just grab this year's top book – the most sought after subjects are timeless enough to justify a look at the older titles as well. You might be surprised at what you can find.

You'll also find the same range of subjects and authors available on audiotapes and compact discs. You can listen to them in your car, on your walkman or on your home stereo – it's a good way to make use of your daily commuting time or just shut out the world around you with earphones.

## Finding The Right Style for You

Depending on your own personal style, you'll find that certain people and topics have a greater impact on you while others do not feel quite right even when they are discussing the exact same topic. Regardless of whether you are looking for a book or a training seminar, you should experiment with various styles in order to find the one with the style and language you can relate to the best.

There are seven basic overlapping categories of self-help and how-to (there are also religious, esoteric, and mystical approaches, but these are beyond the scope of this book). Every category has hundreds, if not thousands of books written from that particular viewpoint. The following examples are some of the more popular books, as you have probably come across at least some of them. Please note that they are given as examples, not recommendations.

*Just the Facts.* This group contains books and other resources which focus only on the factual information of how to do something. Anything from how to ride a mountain bike to growing flowers to interviewing job applicants can be found here. There is a fine line between what is considered self-development and what is not. You'll find advice on how to acquire specific skills or knowledge and you'll also find material for all levels of expertise. For example, there are guides for beginners as well as very advanced material which will only benefit those who are committed to spending time and making the effort to learn all the fine details. Usually few, if any, issues are raised regarding psycho-logical issues such as human motivation, beliefs and attitudes. An example of a self-help book in the "just the facts" category would be Kirsten Lagatree's *Checklists for Life: 104 Lists to Help You Get Organized, Save Time, and Unclutter Your Life.*

***Business How-to.*** Ranging from teamwork training to the memoirs of ex-industry captains (e.g. Jack Welch, *Jack: Straight from the Gut*), this group is aimed at anybody who wants to get ahead in their career or improve their business. What makes it different from other business titles is that it speaks directly to you and shares experiences, tips and hints at a personal level instead of presenting impressive strategies or economic analysis. One of the many bestsellers in this category is Harvey Mackay's business how-to guide *Swim With the Sharks Without Being Eaten Alive.*

***Popular Science.*** This includes those practitioners in the area of counseling, psychology and the medical profession as well as a wide range of academics who want to reach a more general audience. Often based on years of experience and research, these books can become permanent household names (*Doctor Atkins' Diet*, for example) or be a brief flash in the pan, only to quickly return the author or speaker back to relative obscurity. Use of scientific research to make a point naturally extends to almost all of the seven basic categories mentioned, but here it features most prominently. However, many people with Ph.D. or MD titles don't actually write directly about their own area of expertise. Their degrees feature prominently on book covers because pub-lishers find that it lends the work a reassuring aura of credibility.

*Motivational.* Also known as the "you can do anything" category, it guides you to reach your goals and proposes that there are virtually no limits to what you can be, have or do. Dealing with aspects such as goal setting, the power of the mind, self-motivation and managing and overcoming life's obstacles, this category of books focuses on the psychological side of success. Some have developed very elaborate methodologies and strategies, while others focus more on inspirational stories of human achievement. Examples range from classics like Dale Carnegie's famous *How to Win Friends and Influence People*, to modern works such as *Awaken the Giant Within* by Anthony Robbins.

*Life Management.* Very similar to the motivational category, it includes a wide range of advice on taking control of your life: finding out what you really want to do, making a personal plan, improving your self-esteem or dealing with losses and disappointments. The basic idea is that there are "life skills" that are not taught at school or acquired from parents, and by learning these skills we can do better and be happier. An example would be Barbara Sher's book *I Could Do Anything If I Just Knew What It Was.*

*Relationships and Parenting.* Anything from finding a partner to improving your love life to raising kids forms the central theme of these works. When you want to learn more about attraction, love, separation or similar emotions having to do with your loved ones, the authors and trainers in this area offer their help. Famous titles include John Gray's *Men Are from Mars, Women Are from Venus*, which has turned into a whole series of books on different aspects of relationships. Other examples are Laura

Schlessinger's *Ten Stupid Things Couples Do to Mess Up Their Relationships* and Phillip McGraw's *Relationship Rescue.*

*Soul and Spirit.* This is about finding your life's true journey and connecting with yourself. Dealing with your heart's desires, this category offers balance and consolation to those who feel torn between their careers, families, hectic life styles and personal aspirations. Often spiritual in nature, it can be too touchy-feely for some, while other people find these ideas at the very center of their lives. Books in this category include for example Scott Peck's *The Road Less Traveled* or Mitch Albom's *Tuesdays with Morrie.*

## Authors and Trainers

There are thousands of books that promise to reveal to you the secrets of successful businesses, happy relationships, perfect memory, fast weight-loss or anything else you could possibly imagine. Thousands of personal development coaches from around the country offer you their help and expertise in a number of fields. There has never been a better time to find out how to attain or how to become virtually anything you desire.

Some authors have written books in their spare time, coincidentally being one of the few people in the world who has learned lessons of teamwork and leadership from years of being a professional mountaineer trying to reach the summit of Mount Everest, for example. On the other hand, other authors have struggled for years to turn personal coaching into their new full-time profession in a field full of other hopefuls. Some decidedly lack any academic qualifications whatsoever, while others boast Ph.D. and MD degrees from famous universities. However, most of them remain known only to a small group of people in their special areas of expertise, with only a handful ever achieving nationwide publicity and popularity.

Because there are so many authors and speakers, it is impossible to begin to list anything but a few examples (for more, please refer to the resource list at the end of the book). Their individual styles and approaches vary widely, but it does not matter whether we call them authors, speakers, teachers, mentors, coaches or gurus. What matters is that they possess knowledge, skills and methods that they can pass on to you that will help you achieve what you want. They will motivate you, act as your sparring partner and inspire you to make a change in your life.

A famous name or a fancy title does not guarantee that the person is better equipped to help you than someone you have never heard of. A bestseller does not necessarily contain better advice than what is found in an obscure book. To be fair, it must be said that if a person can make a decades-long career out of giving advice, there usually is something more concrete to his or her message than just good presentation and marketing skills. However, should someone appear for a short time and then disappear, it is not necessarily a sign that their message was somehow insignificant or unimportant. In our ever-increasing desire for something new and fresh, it is often the case that many books are simply overlooked or discounted, and their messages do not receive all the publicity or attention they deserve.

You need to exercise your own judgment at all times regarding who you listen to. However, as explained in the previous chapter, at the beginning the most important thing is simply to begin. Just paying attention to what you do is going to produce results. Get yourself started rather than becoming absorbed in the search for the perfect book or coach. What often matters most is that you become aware of what's going on in your present situation and resolve to make a change – finer details can be worked out later. Once you have started, you will be guided to new resources and people, making it much easier to select the best materials.

**Motivational Gurus**

Motivational speakers promise to provide you with the tools to turn your dreams into reality. They teach the principles of human achievement and utilize a wide range of methods, from books to seminars to websites. Selling hundreds of thousands of books and speaking in what is sometimes literally thousands of events, they achieve a "guru status" in their field. This is the highest echelon in what has become the self-help industry.

Famous motivational coaches include the following people: Anthony Robbins, Zig Ziglar, Jim Rohn, Brian Tracy, Denis Waitley, Stephen Covey, Mark Victor Hansen, Jack Canfield and John Gray. These people are sometimes larger-than-life personalities who have developed their individual styles over decades and boast a nationwide fan base. Some radiate energy like a nuclear powerplant (Robbins), some sport the gray hair of years of wisdom (Rohn and Tracy), and some have earned doctorates (Covey and Waitley). Some gurus are down-to-earth, while others have acquired an aura of celebrity. What they all have in common is that they truly believe in their mission and in what they are teaching.

The best and most famous command a price of tens of thousands of dollars for a one-day seminar. Although they might be at the top of their field, they are not necessarily ten times better than the person who steps up to the podium for a fraction of the price. Increasingly, the big name gurus keep earning bigger fees because they are an invaluable marketing tool for the promoter whose aim is to draw big crowds to an event.

It takes years of effort to work your way up to the top where thousands of people gather to hear you speak or flock to buy your latest set of audio tapes. Failing to spark any interest from publishing houses, Mark Victor Hansen and Jack Canfield promoted their self-published book *Chicken Soup for the Soul* for years before a brave publisher finally decided to take the risk and give them a chance. The book subsequently took off like a shot in the mass market and the bookstores became flooded with the bestsellers of the now famous *Chicken Soup* series. But most would-be gurus never make it big in this very competitive market.

There are also clear fashion cycles in the self-help and how-to industry. Sometimes a certain topic becomes so hot that the first people to successfully exploit it instantly become famous household names. Virtually nobody in the general public had ever heard of "emotional intelligence" a few years ago, but Daniel Goleman changed all that in an instant when he coined the term in his huge bestseller book of the same name. Suddenly magazines and TV shows were awash with people discussing the importance of emotional intelligence over traditional IQ. Overnight, Goleman became – willingly or unwillingly – the guru who was flooded with requests to speak at various seminars. On the other hand, certain topics are always in fashion. Sales coaching is a steady seller, and people are always interested in anything having to do with relationships and dieting.

Self-development is clearly a business, not particularly that different from private clinics and doctors who also charge you a fee to help you to improve your life. Many people find that they are willing to buy a certain book or attend a special workshop if it will bring them a little closer to getting what they want out of life.

## But How Can They Know Everything?

It is easy to understand how a top basketball coach might write a book about teamwork and how a practicing child therapist might offer advice on raising mentally healthy children. What raises eyebrows, however, are the people who appear to master a seemingly endless range of subjects. Anything from motivation to sales success, from raising kids to better sex, from vibrant health to financial freedom – these peole will show you how to do it! Surprisingly, sometimes there is a valid reason for this.

First, the same basic principles of achievement apply across the board. You always need to establish your goals, learn from the experts, devise a plan, take decisive action, believe you will succeed, keep trying, and so on. With little modification, you can often extend the same basic ideas to all human activity.

Second, many trainers have mastered the skill of continuous learning. They are always further developing their programs, so it is natural for them to incorporate new areas into their teaching. Remember, many of them have been doing this for decades – they did not make up all this stuff overnight!

The third reason is that personal development coaches are not only effective at simplifying and communicating knowledge, but also at how to turn it into action which leads to results. They are not necessarily experts in a given content matter (they use outside help as well), but they are experts at extracting the key points, breaking them into action steps and then organizing them into a logical process. On top of that, they present their message vividly and with conviction, affirming that anybody can follow this process to get the results they want.

Sometimes we may find that the speakers and authors are not completely up-to-date regarding the latest knowledge in their fields. However, what is often more important than the latest scientific details is the following: what is the meaning behind it all. You need someone to relate or connect new ideas to what you already know, providing a basis for structuring, organizing and interpreting new information as it comes along. It may not be so much about how to invest your money in today's market conditions, but rather why you should invest, what kind of outcome you can expect, what the process consists of, and what you need to know. In essence, the sense of it all.

When you are drowning in information, the most valuable thing somebody can teach you is how to organize it all, interpret it and turn it into action. In effect, what self-help and how-to authors and speakers are doing is speeding up the creation of knowledge structures that would take you years to come up with yourself without guidance. Once you begin to develop these structures for yourself it is easy to attach or add all the new information you want. You should never accept all the self-help ideas as a given without examining them first, but very few of us have thought about all these issues in detail. You can benefit greatly from someone who can provide you with the key ideas in a structured, organized manner.

## What If You've Already Heard It All Before?

Many self-development ideas, no matter who they come from, may not seem new or original because the fact is, they aren't. Some lessons have been amongst us for thousands of years. That does not make them any less relevant today, however.

We are a culture that is obsessed with the new and innovative; we always want the latest developments. But when it comes to self-help, there is very little that has changed about human beings over the past hundred years. Therefore, trainers shouldn't be expected to reinvent the wheel. Instead, ask them how to apply the proven and time-tested idea of the "wheel" in new and innovative ways. It doesn't matter that the authors and speakers didn't discover most of the things they are teaching – just because your history teacher did not discover the dinosaurs didn't make it any less impressive to hear about them.

Good books and good trainers are those that get you interested and exited about a subject, who make it possible to understand new ideas by relating them to your experiences and your existing knowledge. This is why metaphors are so often used in self-help and how-to materials. By using a metaphor you can find common ground to which you can relate new ideas. Most people will know what you mean when you make a connection between an example and the idea behind it. And, even when someone does not immediately grasp what is being said, at least they do not feel excluded by difficult terminology or a lack of special knowledge. Personal development coaches do not use sports teams as metaphors to describe teamwork because they are obsessed with sports. They use them because everybody can grasp the meaning.

The best teachers are those who embody their message. They

live and breathe what they preach. They set a personal example
and encourage you to take action. This matters a great deal
because human experience encompasses much more than simply
an intellectual grasp of ideas; emotions play a major part in everything we do, too. When you feel energized by someone, when you
feel that the person speaks your language so to speak, then you
know you have found the right trainer for you, even if the
content of their message consists of nothing new.

## Focus on the Message, Not the Messenger

Sometimes it is useful to let the person delivering the message
simply fade into the background and focus on the message instead.
Arnold Schwarzenegger has been quoted by saying that during
his highly successful early career as a professional body-builder,
he was willing to take advice from absolutely anyone, including
the "pencil-necks" at the gym who were obviously not as well
trained as he was. What mattered more was that the advice made
sense to him; it was not important who the person was who was
giving him the advice. Yet we often forget this when there is
something about the appearance of the speaker or author that
rubs us the wrong way.

Something that you may find irritating is an overly-positive
attitude. When we are not confident in our abilities we do not
take action, which is why the motivational speakers try to motivate us by telling us that there are absolutely no limits and that
we can do absolutely anything. However, most people are not
looking to change every aspect of their lives; they are just hoping
to improve certain areas. In such an instance, promising solutions
which allow you to have "the perfect life" can actually take some
credibility away from the trainer. Although they mean well,

sometimes those who try to cheer us on might inadvertently do the opposite by going overboard in their enthusiasm.

The know-it-all attitude which some authors and speakers adopt can also make us less receptive to them. We simply cannot believe that this person is qualified to give advice and offer a success system on a seemingly endless range of subjects. We know that the same basic principles apply to almost any subject, but there are a few authors and speakers who spread themselves too thin by being willing to give advice on just about anything.

Sometimes we may question whether the person is qualified or not. Many of the self-help trainers lack higher academic qualifications. However, formal qualifications do not necessarily ensure that the person is more legitimate than someone without them. What matters is whether the person is knowledgeable about the subject, is able to express their ideas in a clear way, and inspires and leads us to take action.

Another way we question a person's qualifications is by comparing them directly to the most successful people in their particular field. Unfairly, we think that because the speaker is not the CEO of a multibillion dollar company, he or she could not possibly give valuable advice to these companies. What we tend to forget is that very few sports coaches could actually play on the teams they coach, yet they are invaluable in terms of analysis, training methods and strategy. And conversely, very few former professional athletes can make good coaches after their careers. Coaching is a special skill, very different from actually performing the task itself.

Finally, what can also irritate us are the authors or speakers who directly challenge our beliefs and ideas. They do this in order to snap our brains out of autopilot mode and get us to really think about the ideas that we normally hold true. Combined with something about a speaker's outer appearance or their manner of speaking, you may become skeptical. (You have a right to be, otherwise anybody could fool you and you would be gullible.) However, new ideas tend to come precisely from those people who are not quite like us. So take a moment to consider *what* someone has to say, not *who* is saying it. You do not have to say "yes" or "no" to an idea right away, just take some time to consider it. Remember Arnold's advice: separate the message from the messenger.

# Sifting Through the Psychobabble

According to self-help and how-to advice, your self-motivation, beliefs, values and habits are more important in terms of achieving your goals than anything else. Getting what you want in life depends more on your inner world than your outer circumstances. How does it all work? Why do these things hold such power over the outcome of your efforts? And what do you do if all the talk about the subconscious mind and the power of belief sounds like useless psychobabble?

Beliefs and values construct your idea of the world. They give you a sense of direction and help you to decide what is true and what is false. You believe that the sky is not going to fall on your head, that your heart will continue to beat and that there will be a tomorrow. You believe hundreds of other things as well, and attach all kinds of values (good, bad, desirable, etc.) to various thoughts, events and people in your life. These are, if you will, the programs that your mind uses to operate. We all have them, and their role is to guide us in our actions and thoughts.

Because this is not stored in our active or conscious mind, we are often not aware of everything that guides us. Sometimes we may even hear someone claim, "I don't believe in anything." This is not true, because without beliefs you would not know what to do and you would become paranoid (just try discarding the belief that you'll automatically continue breathing while sleeping, a belief we all share, and you'll be in big trouble).

Beliefs, values, identity and other terms are not psychobabble that you can ignore – they are very real and affect absolutely everybody. They are simple to understand and offer a great deal of insight into why you do things the way you do and how you could improve.

## Beliefs and Values Drive You

Beliefs are assumptions based on certain information that you hold to be true. In that sense, your beliefs are your reality. Whatever you believe is true to you. Your beliefs make you take action, and as action leads to consequences, it is through your belief system that the brain interprets what is happening to you. Your beliefs may turn out to be true or false, depending on whether you have correct or incorrect information to support them. Sometimes you may not even have much information, yet you still believe in something very strongly. What matters most is that it feels very real to you.

What does all this have to do with self-development? Your mind operates under whatever assumptions (beliefs) you hold to be true. If you believe that you can do something, or if you believe that you cannot, then that's the way it will usually end up. If you believe that you cannot lose weight or that you cannot go higher than middle-management during your career, then that is exactly how things will in all likelihood turn out. Your actions will reflect your beliefs, whether those beliefs have any basis in reality or not.

If beliefs are nothing but assumptions that we hold to be true, it is easy to see what can go wrong. Your beliefs may be limiting your potential. You may not take the right kind of action because you don't believe it will lead to results. When you believe that your beliefs about the world are the truth instead of a collection of assumptions, you will be reluctant to consider other ideas. You may disregard certain actions altogether because they are not supported by your belief system. More problematic yet, you are often not even aware of your beliefs because they affect you at a subconscious level. But whether you realize it or not, they guide and influence all of your actions.

Most people hold some contradictory beliefs. You could believe that anyone can become a success by working hard, but at the same time you believe that this does not apply to you since you are not intelligent enough. Contradictory beliefs cause discomfort and stress because while one belief is guiding us towards something, another belief is causing us to shun or avoid the very same thing. Whatever we do in this particular situation, we are not completely satisfied with the outcome because somewhere in the back of our minds is a nagging feeling that what we did was not completely right or deserved.

What is true about beliefs is largely true about values. Values help you to navigate around our surrounding world. They are the compass that helps you get oriented so you can see where you are going. You must have a strong sense of direction, otherwise the thousands of competing and contradictory signals from the environment will distract you. To break free from the bombardment of messages you must have a clear internal sense of direction which is sustained by your values about right and wrong, good and bad, and about how things should be ideally. As with beliefs, you have not always consciously chosen many of your values, rather you have acquired them from your environment over the years and have accepted them as self-evident. When you want to improve your life, you must improve your values first because they set the stage for everything else.

Your beliefs and values are your mind's autopilot, functioning even when you are not consciously thinking about it. This is helpful because it makes your mental processes more efficient. But problems can arise if the "programming" of the autopilot no longer suits your needs, or if somebody else did the programming for you and you do not know how to change what has already been programmed. You can let your autopilot take over as long as you take charge of your autopilot. For this reason, so much of self-help and how-to deals with how to trigger a change in your beliefs. When you change your beliefs, you can change the process that drives you.

When you become aware of the beliefs you hold to be true, you can begin to understand and consciously control what your actions or inactions are based on. The point is not, however, to think about our beliefs all the time. What you want to avoid is "paralysis by analysis," where you spend all your time analyzing rather than taking action. Even when some of our beliefs are contradictory (as they are bound to be), or when something we believe in is downright wrong (it happens), we are still empowered to act. And action alone will give us productive feedback from the real world.

The first step is to recognize and remind yourself of the power of your belief and value systems. You can then move towards examining them systematically with a good book or a seminar.

## If I Believe Hard Enough, Will It Become Reality?

Well, yes and no. Believing in itself will not make things materialize; only the action you take, based on your beliefs, can advance you towards your goals. What is also very important to realize, and something that you can misunderstand from a quick glance at a self-help book, is that rarely is a single belief alone responsible for your success or lack of it.

All your beliefs together form a belief system. You normally seek to add new beliefs or refine the old based on how they fit into the belief system as a whole that you have created. You tend to adopt those that fit and discard those that do not. You may even interpret the outcome of certain events in a way which supports your beliefs, although in reality it is pointing to something in the opposite direction. You do this to keep your belief system coherent and to protect the internal logic that you have established. In addition, your beliefs must also be socially acceptable to you. You do not have to conform to *all* the standards of the society around you, but a certain amount of shared or common beliefs is necessary in order for you to operate and get along with other people. Therefore, you simply cannot perform the magic trick of planting a belief in your head that claims you will be hugely successful in everything you do and expect it to become reality with the wave of a magic wand! This would clash with the other beliefs in your system and the "evidence" that you have that points in the other direction. It would also clash with what the society around us believes.

It has been said that you can only become what you already

believe. Your belief system tends to gather momentum that moves you in a certain direction (or, if you have many contradictory beliefs, tends to keep you put and allows very little movement in any direction). You tend to reinforce those beliefs that are in accordance with what you already believe and discard any conflicting beliefs. This means that to get the full power of your beliefs working for you, you need to change many more than just one. Believing that you can be the top salesperson in your company is a start. But unless you *also* believe that you must change the way you do things and take action, that you must begin immediately and work both hard and smart, it is difficult to get enough momentum for real changes to take place.

One belief is a start and something you can build upon. In conjunction with other interconnected and supporting beliefs, it will work wonders.

## Normative Values in Self-Help

The society around us and the people close to us often exert gentle (or not so gentle) pressure to conform to the values they hold to be "right." Self-help can offer a way to examine those normative values and to understand whether they support you or hold you back from becoming what you want to become. But self-help books and trainers also have normative values which they promote in many ways and which should be examined a little more closely before adopting.

Optimism and positive thinking, belief in progress and action orientation, trust in techniques and methods are typical examples of values espoused in self-improvement. Experience may well have shown that these lead to results and therefore are to be encouraged. But that does not mean they should all be taken at face value.

Consider optimism and positive thinking, for example. Certainly, these attitudes make you more willing to try things out, helping to expand your abilities. But you should not completely disregard the other side of the coin, the power of negative emotions. Feeling bad, being angry and other negative emotions can spur you to action as much as optimism can. Negative aspects can be a constructive force, something that will provide equilibrium. Negative emotions are also something you need to understand in order to relate to other people who will continue to have these emotions, no matter what outlook you ultimately choose to adopt for yourself.

Normative values, wherever they come from, often exclude rather than include. Being too absolute can cause you to fail to see the big picture. Take some time to think them through, no matter how "right" they feel or who is presenting them to you.

## Certainty and Confidence

Another central concept in self-improvement is that when you feel certain about something and when you have the confident expectation that things will turn out well for you, then that is what will happen. Whether positive or negative, you create your outer world from your inner world. This is largely true because expecting a certain outcome helps you to tune your attention to things that will move you towards it. It also encourages you to interpret what is happening as something that conforms to your expectations, thus "proving" to you that you are on the right track.

Feelings of certainty and confidence play a big role in being able to make a change. When you feel certain about things, it is easy for you to take action. You feel that you are in control, that you understand what is happening and that you can affect the outcome. Paradoxically, taking confident action, as a consequence, often brings about new circumstances that may in fact lead you to become confused or uncertain. It is precisely because of your confidence that you will encounter a new situation and not know how to deal with it. This is a sign that you are growing and expanding out of your old comfort zone, and once you understand your new circumstances, the confidence comes back and you are ready to take the next step.

Feeling too certain or overly-confident can actually prevent you from taking action and making changes. When you are too certain, you do not feel the need to change; you think you are in control and feel good about it. However, you cannot function as a human being without feeling uncertain at times. If you were sure about everything all the time, you would not question and analyze your actions, nor would you learn from others who have contradictory opinions or information to your own. So the next time you feel uncertain and uncomfortable, understand why this can be good and why it can even be advantageous to welcome some uncertainty in your life.

Feel certain – but at the same time allow yourself to be uncertain. It is the only way to improve, to take new action, and to get new results.

## Identity Is Who You Are

Identity is who you think you are. It is your self-image, your idea of what kind of a person you are. Your identity is based on your beliefs about yourself. Your beliefs can be so strong, and you can hold them to be so self-evident that you will not even want to evaluate them. They are deeply ingrained in your self-identity and guide your decisions and actions, even to the degree that there are some things that you cannot even consider doing because they are so contrary to your idea about the kind of a person you are.

Your identity keeps developing and changing throughout your life, although it usually remains very stable once it has been established. It is formed by interacting with other people, your social and the physical environment, and the interpretations which you attach to what is happening during these interactions. You are what you continuously do, and as you tend to do things that are in line with your identity, your actions produce constant reinforcement.

Your identity is linked to your purpose in life. Whereas goals are more or less concrete objectives you want to reach, your life's purpose is a more abstract idea of what you exist for and what you experience in this world. Your purpose can include becoming a better person, being the soul of your local community, or a thousand other things, but it can also be something that you have never given much consideration to before. Talking about your life's purpose may sound lofty, but it is really about finding out what you love to do and want to do in your life. Whatever it may be, identifying it will allow you to see what the central theme is in your life and give you a better understanding of the person you are.

## Motivation

Motivation is feeling confident that you are moving towards what you want and that this action is in accordance with your beliefs. The prerequisites for motivation include knowing what you want (this doesn't have to be detailed), believing that there are ways of getting what you want, and the feeling that these ways are not in conflict with your values or beliefs. This means that when you are motivated, you know that you are able to and want to do something that will move you closer to your goals. You also know that the methods you are using to get there are what you believe to be right and justified.

Let's say you want to lose weight. To feel motivated to do this, you need to believe that losing weight is what you really want to do and that it will benefit you in some way, and that it is possible for you to achieve this. If you want to lose weight because of fashion or because it has become trendy to do so, or if you are not convinced of the benefits of losing weight, you are naturally not going to be very motivated to try. Nor will you be motivated if you believe that you don't have the discipline. Another example could be wanting more money. You know that you could get rich by robbing a bank, but since this would (hopefully) be clearly against your beliefs and values, you would not be motivated to do this, even if someone were to present you with a foolproof plan for how to go about it. To be really motivated to earn more money, you have to believe that you can figure out a feasible plan; you know that you are capable of this, and that the method of implementing this plan is in accordance with your beliefs.

Only change motivated and produced within yourself will last. Outside motivation, pressure, or help never works long term if your own commitment is lacking. The good thing is that motivation feeds on itself, creating even more motivation. Once you get going, you will find it easier and easier to stay motivated and do even more than you had initially thought possible.

Sometimes we get confused and claim that nothing motivates

us, but all people are naturally motivated. We all want to feel good, to be happy, to be loved, and to accomplish something in our lives. Our motivation has many outlets: family, friends, community, work, etc. Sometimes we may simply feel that we do not have any time, energy or the means to do what we are naturally motivated to do. Or, we may not even know what we want. In some cases our natural motivation may find a negative outlet and we do things that we later come to regret.

Your motivation is driven by your beliefs. Your beliefs can either support you or they can limit you. You may, for example, be motivated to stay just the way you are, although you would like to get something more out of life. How can this be? Your beliefs tell you that although you would like to change, it is dangerous; it may bring failure and it may not work at all, leading to wasted efforts and perhaps even ridicule. If you believe that by not changing you will be safe, you will be motivated to keep things as they are. Not only does this hinder your ability to improve the situation, it also creates frustration because your wants and beliefs are pulling you in two opposite directions.

## Why Feelings Matter

Why do feelings matter? Can't you just get to the core of any old "success method" and skip all this touchy-feely stuff about human emotions? The answer is no, because that would be ignoring one of the main reasons we humans function the way we do. Feelings matter tremendously and it is important to understand their place in your self-improvement efforts.

In a sense, everything you want in life is about feelings. You want certain possessions, you want certain relationships, you want certain things to happen – all because of how they make you feel. You are motivated by moving towards certain feelings, or moving away to avoid certain feelings, or by trying to maintain a certain kind of feeling.

Feelings do not come from the outside; they come from the inside. With the exception of direct physical feeling from one of our senses (pain, for example), we do not feel something because of what happens, we feel something because we ourselves create that feeling internally. But feelings are not just in your mind, they are also in your physiology – the way you move, breathe and touch. By involving your mind and body, you can feel any way you want without any external reason.

Understanding the importance of feelings does not necessarily mean that your number one priority has to be "getting in touch with your feelings." Some people have a world view that makes them slightly uncomfortable with lots of talk about feelings. If you are one of these people, begin by adopting an intellectual understanding of why feelings matter so much. Dealing with emotions is not the opposite of being rational or in conflict with searching for scientific reasons, it is just another way of looking at how humans function. Ultimately, not being able to deal with your and other people's feelings will limit both your abilities to improve and enjoy the progress you make.

## The Subconscious Mind

The favorite phrase of many self-help authors has long been "tapping into your subconscious mind." This means that you should utilize the part of your brain that automatically processes thoughts and actions without letting them pop up in your conscious thought process. Is this really so important?

The concept of the subconscious mind has a solid scientific

basis – your mind *does* operate at different levels. Unfortunately, there has been no lack of individuals who have claimed to have discovered "hidden subconscious powers" and subsequently have gone on to sell these unbelievable and unlikely ideas to the unsuspecting public. The subconscious mind can surprise you with what it can do, but tapping into it will not make you a mind-reader, give you powers to talk to the dead or get somebody to fall madly in love with you, all of which has been claimed in the name of the subconscious mind. Steer clear of the people who claim that they have discovered abilities nobody else has ever heard of.

The subconscious mind has a great deal of power because your brain likes to automate things in the name of efficiency. There are two key uses of this: letting your subconscious mind automatically steer or guide you, thereby freeing up a lot of mental capacity for other tasks, or letting your subconscious mind process thoughts for you in hopes that it can tap resources that you might not otherwise reach. Your subconscious mind is not something you can choose to switch off at will – it is always going to be there, so it makes sense to get to know it a little better.

## When Diagnosis Is Part of the Cure

Self-help gurus and good consultants have always been aware of the following: the only way their clients are going to get better, and stay that way, is to involve them in finding the cure to the problem. In fact, often the only thing an outside consultant can do is to help the client diagnose the problem. The nature of the "cure" is such that it cannot be removed from the person in question and cannot be performed by someone else. Only the client can take the necessary action, whether it concerns saving a business from bankruptcy or quitting smoking.

A diagnosis is done by asking questions that help you to see the important issues and the relationships between these significant issues. Incidentally, diagnosis is already a step towards solving those issues. By simply getting the issues out into the open, you automatically begin to see possible solutions. The best consultants may not even do the diagnosis – and they certainly do not give you any answers – they just teach you how to go about diagnosing the problem yourself. It works like magic because we are often reluctant to take advice from others, especially when it pertains to what we should be doing. But when you have done the diagnosis yourself, you cannot escape the responsibility of taking action. You are the best expert to solve your own problems.

Interestingly, most people are already aware of the solutions to their problems (this applies to healthy people, some individuals have conditions that need to be treated by experts). You already know what works but this may be exactly why you do not want to believe it. You may need an outsider just to point out the obvious to you, to help you get rid of any excuses you may be making and to confirm that you knew the answer yourself all along.

This is what many how-to and self-help trainers do at their seminars. They begin by having you ask yourself a set of questions which leads to a diagnosis your present situation. After this, the prescription for the action you should take can appear so self-evident that you may wonder why you are paying so much money for this in the first place! You need to realize that the diagnosis itself is part of the cure, and even when it sounds simple, there is a lot of value in having someone guide you through the process and assure you that you are taking the right approach.

You still need to learn to take the right kind of action, and just getting the right diagnosis is in itself not enough to do this, but getting started is always the first step.

## Facing the Truth About Yourself

There is a widely-believed myth in self-help that claims you avoid certain things because you do not want to face the truth about yourself. This is partially true: you tend to avoid things that don't conform to your identity. There is a problem with this idea, however. Avoiding certain things also implies that you have a weak mind because you cannot push yourself past your boundaries or limitations, and furthermore, if you had a stronger sense of self, you could deal with the uncomfortable facts about yourself, thereby rising above and over any limitations you have.

This has led to tremendous amounts of frustration as people think that whenever they fail to learn new concepts or take up new activities, it is because their "weak" minds avoid having to accept the truth. In turn, this then makes them try to control their mind-set even more, only to discover that even by trying very hard, there are still things they cannot bring themselves to do. This does not exactly do wonders for one's self-image. In fact, it makes trying the next time much harder because this individual has now firmly established the belief that he or she is weak-minded.

There is a great mix-up of ideas here. It is true that you cannot bring yourself to do certain things in your life, even when you know it would be good for you. However, it is absolutely untrue that this is because your mind is so weak. Exactly the opposite is true – you cannot tackle certain things because your mind is so strong.

Your mind is trying to preserve its integrity and internal logic by not allowing you to change your way of thinking or discard your boundaries too easily. This integrity allows you to operate. If you constantly changed your way of thinking, you would literally go insane. Consistency is a very strong feature of the human mind. It doesn't make any sense to call it a weakness and blame yourself.

Of course, this mechanism can hinder actual improvement by protecting the status quo too much. However, you will only make it worse if you blame yourself for not having enough control or willpower to overcome it. You cannot totally turn off a part of your mind, and there is no reason to do so. What should you do then? Simply accept it! Accept the fact that your new activity may bring you a little discomfort at first, making your mind protest and making you doubt whether you can do it. When you understand why this happens – a sign that you are a perfectly normal, mentally healthy human being – your ability to deal with this discomfort changes dramatically.

Consider the example of taking up jogging. When your body is not used to this type of activity, it will protest and you'll get sore muscles after the first few attempts. If you are a person who gives up easily, you will either never try jogging in the first place, or after a few attempts, conclude that it is simply not for you. But when you are aware that the first few times are likely to be a little frustrating, you will have modified your expectations to match the reality. When you also have support systems to keep you going (a jogging buddy, for example), and when you give it enough time, you will succeed. The real beauty of this, however, is that what was initially stopping you from jogging in the first place, will in time stop you from giving it up! When jogging has become part of your weekly routine, your mind will strongly protest against stopping because it wants to keep intact your newly-formed identity of "I am a person who jogs."

So yes, you *do* have to push past your limits, otherwise you cannot grow. And yes, you *do* have to take a good look at yourself in the mirror and see which areas you can improve upon. But when you find these things hard to do, remember that is not a sign that you are weak-minded. Accept that not everything is easy, understand why everybody's mind is designed to resist change, and ultimately you will have a much better chance at succeeding in what you want to do.

## Structure Brings Better Results Than Willpower

Skip any self-help program where the discourse is only about self-discipline, willpower and staying sharply focused. There is a good chance that there are some smart and useful strategies lacking that could help in the long run. There's no question about it – you do need to develop your willpower, but it is also important to understand that it is even more critical to enlist the help of those around you; in other words, to create support structures. These support structures will help you hang in there even when you do not have the energy to do it alone.

Forget the idea that everybody else ends up with better results than you because they have more willpower. Nobody has that much willpower. Very few people can "will" their way through absolutely anything and even if they could, this would be very exhausting. For most of us, pure willpower is rarely enough to carry us through a long-term effort.

Once you get yourself moving with that initial burst of energy, the most important thing is to make sure you have the kind of support that will keep you going day after day – even if you yourself don't always feel up to it. The results of self-development will only last when they have been turned into consistent action and habits. In this case, a "support structure" around you will help you much more than any amount of willpower alone.

Let's take an example. Say you don't go to work today because you don't feel like it for some reason. This is what would happen immediately: If you have a spouse or roommate, they'd start wondering what was wrong; later your colleagues would call you; your boss would call you; someone would ask if you needed any help. In the evening your friends might call you. Everybody would be concerned about why you didn't go to work, they would offer to do something or suggest that you see the doctor (a professional helper). Should you refuse to go to work for no apparent reason, you would receive a warning from your workplace, and additional calls from your friends and colleagues. Should you go missing, the police would start a search. People would not stop until the issue was somehow solved. The support structure around you is helping you to stay on the right track.

Contrast the aforementioned example with a typical personal development attempt where you read a book (alone), decide that you are going to change your life (alone, as there is nobody else involved in the decision), and you begin your attempt with high hopes (but alone). You make some progress, then encounter some obstacles (alone), and finally, your efforts slowly falter because you don't have the determination to continue (alone). No wonder you fail! But even worse, you now blame your "lack of will-power" as the reason you didn't succeed. You may never try again because you have convinced yourself that you simply do not have what it takes. Forget about that! It is virtually impossible to stay disciplined if the support structures around you are missing.

Trying to rely only on willpower all the time is like trying to force yourself to stay awake for two days in a row. You are inviting failure. Oh sure, some people can do it, but it is not a very smart thing to do. It is very rarely necessary to do such a thing and it will just wear you down, no matter who you are. Willpower is like a "turbo boost," an extra kick that you can learn to use selectively to complement the support structures, not to replace them.

### What If It Still Sounds Like Psychobabble?

Often, when we are skeptical about the ideas presented by motivational speakers, we are using our skepticism to mask the fact that we are afraid to try out something new. We are afraid to come to the realization that some of our fears may in fact truly exist, and that would be a hard knock to our internalized system of beliefs: "I know these things, and I know who I am. I don't need to change." For example, it is not easy to accept that we can have virtually whatever we want because this immediately raises the question of whether or not we have been wasting our time all these years not getting what we truly desire. So in order to protect ourselves we downplay the whole idea that this could be true.

Concepts like motivation, belief systems, values and identity are the mechanisms that steer our actions. They are for our brain like software is for computers. You are right to protest if someone makes it all sound like complex bits and bytes that you don't understand, but you cannot ignore its importance. You must learn to use the "software" in order to be productive in reaching for your goals.

**6.**

# Tips for Reading, Tapes and Seminars

Some people may think that nobody needs advice on how to read a book, much less on how to watch someone on stage, but reading a how-to book or attending a personal development workshop actually requires a very specific approach. Little things *do* matter. Done consistently over time, they can make a big difference in the outcome. For example, we all have a particular time of the day or night during which we work most productively. Reading and studying how-to books during this time might seem insignificant, and in the time frame of a week or so it won't make much of a difference in your life whether you work at this time or at another time. But if you constantly work during this productive time, you'll get better results than you would if you did your work at whatever time of the day you could find.

Since your time is always limited to 24 hours a day, it makes sense to try to make the most out of it. Many of us acquired our "study habits" a long time ago at school and might need a little brush up.

Picking up new ideas and information is obviously not enough. You need to turn them into action and then know how to maintain that action despite the difficulties that might arise. Let's look at some tips on how to read or listen more effectively and get more out of seminars and training events.

## How to Read Effectively

Tom Peters, after co-authoring with Robert Waterman the biggest business bestseller of the 1980s entitled *In Search of Excellence*, remarked in his next book that although the book had sold over five million copies, perhaps only 100,000 people had read it cover-to-cover, and perhaps only as few as 5,000 people had really taken detailed notes on the book. It is not difficult to guess who out of all those people actually got the most out of the book! So here is how to read most effectively:

**Find time to read.** Plan beforehand when you are going to read. Otherwise, that book or audiotape may become just another source of stress and frustration as you remember that you should have been doing it for weeks now, but have just not found the time. Remember, you usually need at least an hour to get into the book and its particular style. Thirty-minute bursts are too short and more than three hours is usually too long as your concentration starts to wander.

**Read actively.** Work the book. Make notes. Review. Write in the margins. Talk to yourself. Read aloud. Pick out important parts. Scribble. Draw. Underline. Highlight. Circle. Write your own summaries. Think about what applies to your life and work. Feel the feelings. Act as you read (go ahead, nobody is going to be watching you!). Get physical. Move. And do the exercises – don't skip them. Feeling exhausted yet?

**Understand the context and be open to the message.** Read the front and back covers, read the author's biography, read about the sources, and find out more about the topic from the Internet, for example. Put yourself in the mind-set of having "positive expectations" – it will make reading more effective (you can always turn on your critical analysis later). Do not just speak (read) the words in your mind, but also listen to the words in your mind. Think not only in terms of words but also images and feelings.

**Do not read more than two chapters per week.** To increase the effectiveness, reduce the dosage. To learn faster, read slower. Give yourself time to do some of the exercises described in the book. There is so much advice in a good how-to book that if you read it cover-to-cover without taking a break, you cannot possibly internalize it all, much less know how to take action. Slow down, and you will get better results.

**Remember that solutions are simple.** To learn to read fast, read a book on reading fast (but find a balance between speed and understanding).

**Buy a pack of yellow highlighter pens.** Apply generously.

## Reading Tricks

There are a number of small reading tricks to break the routine and help you become "unstuck" in your efforts. They can help you to find the energy to finish that chapter, give you new perspectives and make reading more fun. They are not meant to be used all at the same time or followed every time you read. Try some of them the next time you pick up a book.

**Close, close, closer:** Put the book really close to your face, so that the letters seem big and you can smell the ink. Then begin to read those few important pages again. You'll notice how intensive the reading experience is.

**Check the punctuation:** Become aware of the punctuation. A period is different from a question mark. When you come to a question mark, stop and think. What is it really there for? Repeat the question out loud if you want, and then remember that it was directed to you. So, go ahead and answer it!

**Second wind:** Sometimes we feel that we do not have the energy to go any further. Do not give up, keep going with the book and you have a good chance of getting what runners call their "second wind" – the new rush of energy that suddenly materializes.

**Chuck the book:** If the book really *is* no good, physically throw it on the floor and let it lay there. Admit that it was bad and you do not need to waste your time on it. After you come back from doing something else for a while, pick the book up off the floor and consider whether or not it contained anything of value to you. If yes, you can make a note of those parts; if not, you can really just throw the book away.

**Read someplace new:** We all tend to read at home. Go read a book in the early hours in your workplace, read the book at the library, or read the book outside. Break your routine.

**Read it aloud:** Go ahead, read it aloud. It is funny how different the same book will feel when read aloud. Even old and familiar books take on a whole new feeling.

**Get physical:** Mental and physical conditions are interlinked. Take a break from reading and get some physical exercise. Even better, make the important points in the book stand out by linking them to physical activity – then your whole body will remember instead of just your mind.

**Actively interlink:** While reading, make a point of thinking actively at the end of each chapter about which other lessons are relevant or "linked" to what you have just learned. Write down these "connections" at the end of each chapter. When you process the information in this way, you will internalize it much better.

**Reduce and summarize:** At the end of each page, think about how you would summarize that page in one or two sentences. If you want, write them down.

**Pose a question:** Ask yourself before reading: What question does this book or this chapter provide an answer for? You will subsequently "see" the text answer the question for you, driving home the key points that the author is trying to make.

**Read hard stuff:** Take a book that you would normally consider too difficult to read, such as a book on philosophy. Then plough through a few chapters. Now when you go back to your "regular" reading, it will seem relatively easy.

**Read aloud with a friend:** This is a little scary because your friend might think that this is just plain weird. But if you can do it, you may have just cured your fear of publicly discussing self-improvement ideas. Because it is frightening, it works very effectively. Your senses are at a heightened state and you can feel the impact of the spoken words.

## Audiotapes and Videos

You can learn the same things from a video or an audiotape that you could learn from a book, but the experience is different. You will be using different senses and letting somebody else dictate the pace. It will be easier to understand the tone and experience the feelings – all contributing to the impact of ideas and concepts presented.

Some people sneer at tapes, thinking that they are somehow inferior to printed text. Certainly the higher education system almost exclusively uses books, missing out on some of the benefits of other mediums (why this is, nobody has been able to explain). But if thousands of people have used their commuting time more effectively by listening to tapes in the car or have become infected by some of the trainer's enthusiasm by watching a video, you, too, should give it a try.

However, there is a catch. You may be so used to listening to music and watching movies that out of habit you approach the self-development tapes and videos the same way. Unfortunately, this won't work; it will just turn the presentation into infotainment where you keep nodding your head in agreement to whatever the speaker says, yet in the end remember relatively little.

You're used to reading a book in several sittings but you are not accustomed to pausing a tape at least twenty times before you get to the end. Yet this is exactly what you need to do. Sure, you can go through it all in one go the first time around, but then you need to pause, rewind, take notes, pause again and think (please don't do all this while driving). Use the same study habits you would use for books and you will get optimal results. If you are wondering where to begin, refer to the end of this book for a list of audio and video resources you might want to have a look at.

## The Benefits of Live Events

Live events open up new channels of communication, making the impact more powerful and memorable. Even if the content is similar to the book you have just read, it can really be an eye-opening experience.

Seminars, workshops and training camps are events where the speaker or trainer goes through a predetermined program for one or two days. These events range from training seminars held for a few dozen people to megaevents where the audience numbers in thousands. Traditionally, workshops provided more room for interaction, were shorter in duration and the size of the group was smaller. However, nowadays the two words "workshop" and "seminar" are synonymous, and there is often no difference in content. Here are some reasons you should consider going to a seminar or a workshop:

### Immersion effect

Being exposed to the message for a full day makes it much more intensive than simply reading a book for a couple of hours. You will become totally immersed in the subject matter.

### New environment

Getting away from your normal surroundings and meeting people you would not normally meet is stimulating.

### Audience support

You realize that you are not alone, that other people are in the same boat and have the same types of questions. And as the day progresses, the other participants are usually genuinely willing to offer you their support.

*Trying new things*

Seminars are not just about information, they often include individual and group exercises. The speaker, together with the audience's support, can encourage you to do things you normally would not think about doing or dare to do. The environment is safe for controlled experiments, just enough to get you to step out of your normal comfort zone. You are also required to do things immediately, so you can't postpone them and lose the momentum.

*Enhanced learning*

You are using senses you do not use while reading a book or listening to an audiotape. Ideas presented in conjunction with demonstrations, movement, tone of voice, expressions and feelings can all add tremendously to your learning experience. Much more can be communicated and demonstrated in a live setting than through a book, and the exercises take on a whole new meaning when you find yourself going through them with a total stranger.

*Interaction*

The chance to ask questions and receive immediate clarification is a powerful learning tool. You will become aware of new points of view thanks to other people's questions and you'll have the chance to open up a dialogue on important issues.

*Taking time for yourself*

Going to a full weekend seminar, for example, gives you the sense that you are treating yourself to something special. You are learning and experiencing something important and you are doing it for your own personal reasons. Taking action gives you momentum and builds your confidence.

## How to Attend a Live Event

To prepare yourself for a seminar, first determine what it is you want to achieve. It is not enough just to attend the seminar – you have to actively use the event to further your own goals. You must know what you have come for and be active about getting it. Get yourself in the right mood by going through related material just before the event.

At the venue, don't sit with your friends or colleagues. You already know them. Use the experience to meet new people. Yes, it can be scary, but you will learn more. Besides, when it comes time for the exercise in which you have to to spill your heart's true desires to the person sitting next to you, you'll want to be as far away from your colleagues as possible! (Or then again, maybe not.)

Actively take notes. Don't rely on prepared material only – there is always something mentioned that will be missing from the handouts. Your own notes are the only way to review what was being said.

Review the material after the event. The sooner you do this, the more you will remember. Evaluate whether the event was a good investment for you or not. If it was, immediately resolve to book yourself for the next one before your enthusiasm fades. If you clearly got more out of the event than you invested – time, money, effort – then the only rational decision is to immediately book yourself for two more future events! Think of it as an investment in yourself.

## Looking Silly and Acting Strange

People generally feel very positive about your efforts to learn something new. But starting to follow a self-improvement program can still bring criticism from others. In some form or another it may come from your spouse, friends or fellow workers. Suddenly sporting a bunch of books or tapes is bound to create interest and spur comments – both welcome and unwelcome. If you think that some of the attention is unfair, revisit Chapter 2 to dispel some common misconceptions regarding self-help and how-to. However, it is not all about misconceptions; it is likely that there are real changes in your behavior that are causing people to react this way. Don't let it disturb you, it is a sign that you are making progress.

First, you may look a little silly. You may look a bit strange to someone catching you doing the different exercises described in the how-to books or talking to yourself aloud. This is OK. Whoever said you could not play around a little? People may think that children look somewhat silly when they play, but nobody thinks that they have gone out of their minds. Just because you are an adult does not mean that you are not allowed to be playful, which is actually one of the best ways to learn. Which is better: using all available means to learn and improve your life, or not doing anything because somebody might think you are behaving differently?

Second, you may not be able to convincingly explain exactly what is so wonderful about what you are doing. As well as looking silly, we often sound confused in our reasoning and logic when we are learning. We ourselves may not even be very convinced of the merits of what we are doing. This is a perfectly normal part of the learning process. It can be compared to somebody trying to learn to play the piano. You are not going to sound very good at the beginning, but practicing, even when you can't play very well, is the only way to get better. At the beginning confusion can be a sign that you are developing new ways of looking at things. Simply because you cannot offer a watertight argument in defense of your every action is neither a sign that you don't know what you are doing nor a sign that there is something wrong with the advice. Have a little faith at the beginning and you will see that eventually everything forms a coherent picture.

Third, you may receive all kinds of negative feedback. People do not necessarily mean to discourage you, but they often sense that you are changing and may feel slightly threatened. Tell them that you are trying a few new things, and in doing so you may behave a little differently. Assure them that you are not going to turn into a completely different person and that you still care about them. Then go on with what you are trying to achieve in your life.

## Take a Break

Once in a while you need to take a break because some things only work when given enough time. You cannot squeeze them all into your busy schedule and even if you could, it would not work. Your mind is somewhere else. You need to take some time off.

The modern world seems to move in fast forward. The media, our colleagues and friends all bombard us with messages. Often all you can do is quickly scan the information and move on. But if you never stop, you cannot begin to make sense of it all. Getting more information will not make you more effective or wiser. What you really need is less and better quality – but quality does not work in a hurry.

You have to work with information to turn it into knowledge and wisdom. This is what many of us fail to do, not appreciating the difference between being exposed to information and really processing it. We need time to create new knowledge, to see the interconnections between things and to understand how to apply what we know.

If you feel that you are just turning pages of self-help books and not really internalizing what you read, then perhaps it is time to take a break. Stop for a while. Pick a long weekend, take that book with you and spend some unhurried time with it. The reading experience will be markedly different.

## Checklist: Get the Basics Right

Follow this checklist to get the basics right regardless of whether you are reading, listening or attending a live event:

**At your convenience: Ponder these questions for a while**

- Ask yourself: What do I know about the given subject? Where did I learn this information? Am I aware of any holes there may be in my knowledge? Why is this subject important to me?

**Beforehand: Prepare a little (but not too much)**

- Make learning a top priority or other things will absorb the available time.
- Stop and relax. Even one minute is enough to clear your mind and relax your body. This is supposed to be fun and useful, so it is worth stopping for.
- Manage your expectations. What is the topic, who is the author or speaker, and what is their approach?

- Think about why you are doing this and then resolve to get those results.
- Don't only keep your eyes and ears open, but your mind open, too.
- Prepare to use your feelings, as they will serve as powerful memory cues.

### During: Let it flow (but do take notes)

- See how you can involve not only your thoughts but also your senses: your state of mind, and physical feelings. The more senses you activate, the easier it is to recall and reproduce the ideas later.
- Try to get the big picture and understand the main issues. It is not the words but the point made and the key ideas that matter.
- Think on paper. Take notes as you go along. They will serve as references to which you can come back to later.
- Don't edit or discard any material at this stage. It will distract you and you may miss some things that later turn out to be useful.

### Afterwards: Make it your own

- Make the material your own. Turn it into something that works for you and that has special meaning. Go over it again and make some new notes.
- Review and repeat the material to make the ideas stick.
- Try to understand the material instead of learning it by rote. The "Ah-ha!" experience has power.
- Ponder the meaning with the intention of making connections and associations with what you already know.

- Group the message into chunks that will help you remember it.
- Try to apply the ideas to different situations so that they are reinforced by being relevant in a wide range of circumstances.
- You cannot remember everything nor should you – paper will do that job nicely. But do try to memorize the key points.
- Allow time to assimilate the ideas until you can express them in your own words.
- Keep your notes in sight. As the old saying goes, "Out of sight, out of mind."
- Always turn the ideas into concrete actions. It is the best way to make the lesson really stick.

# PART TWO

# WHY SELF-IMPROVEMENT FAILS AND HOW TO SUCCEED

# Here's Why You Failed Before

The second part of this book explains why people fail in their personal improvement attempts, cautions against common pitfalls and provides practical strategies to deal with inevitable obstacles.

We all have had the following experience: we read a great book or listen to an excellent presentation, we get all charged up about the changes we are going make in our life, we feel really motivated, take a few initial steps and then, despite our best efforts to make it all happen, we fail. And let's face it, even when it has become popular for self-development gurus to claim that you never *really* fail, that this is only a chance to discover what really doesn't work, it *still* feels like a failure. You already know that something went wrong when that diet failed, when you lost that promotion or when you could not hold that relationship together.

When you follow someone's advice and things end up going

wrong, you begin to look for the reasons why. What you usually come up with are the two things that can go wrong in a situation: either the advice you received was wrong or bad advice or your action was not the best action to take. So, it is either the author's/speaker's fault or your own fault that everything did not work out as promised.

Many motivational speakers and authors strongly claim that their teachings are guaranteed to work, but only if you follow their advice correctly and with the right amount of involvement. While this certainly may be true, it also easily shifts the blame onto you. It is certainly not very motivating to hear, "There's nothing wrong with the advice, you just didn't work hard enough." On the other hand, if you think the failure was your own fault, you will feel guilty and bad about it, and since you do not want to feel this way for long, you'll stop your efforts at self-development or begin to blame the advice, which leads to the same outcome. If you think the problem is that the advice is somehow inadequate and the same thing happens several times, you'll lose your belief that any self-help or how-to program could ever really work for you.

Neither fact is of any help to you. If you blame yourself for the failure, the game is over – because why would you bother to try again? If you blame the "bad" advice, the game is over as well – because why would you ever want to waste your time again? Or worse, how are you ever going to find out if it really was the bad advice and not you or your actions after all that led to failure?

Now you are really stuck.

There is a way out of this dilemma, however. It is the realization that often neither the author nor the reader is at fault.

## You Are Not the Reason You Failed Before

Stop punishing yourself. Neither you nor the advice is the real problem.

What *is* the real problem then?

The real problem is that how-to and self-help books come without proper instructions on how to use them. That is why you fail.

Amazingly, the very books, tapes and seminars that are supposed to be instructive contain very little or no information on how to actually get the most out of them. They assume that all they need to do is provide you with a set of how-to rules, principles and inspirational stories all packaged into a step-by-step format, and then suddenly you will just somehow know...

...how to learn the new information effectively,

...how to integrate all the new information into
   your present knowledge, skills and beliefs,

...how to apply the advice to your unique life situation,

...how to translate the steps into a set of consistent
   actions,

...how to analyze the real-life feedback you receive as a
   result of your actions and then adjust your approach
   accordingly.

These steps are far from easy to take, especially if you've never done anything like it before. In fact, they are not necessarily very simple even if you have had some previous experience. Without proper advice on how to go about it, good results are just not likely to happen.

## How-To Comes Without A How To

In most cases you failed because nobody told you how to use the advice given in self-help and how-to books, tapes and seminars. Perhaps the authors or speakers themselves were not aware that there is a need for this kind of knowledge because what they are teaching or instructing may come so naturally to them. They simply may not have thought that people need to know *how* to learn their material, and not just *what* can be learned from their material.

The problem is compounded by the fact that there can simply be too much advice in the average self-help book. There are so many things involved that your mind gets confused and bogged down trying to remember what to do instead of focusing on the actual action itself. Your mind is just not designed to process so much information at one go. The situation becomes even more difficult because the advice you receive is usually fairly generic. It is rarely tailored to your unique situation so your brain works overtime trying to adapt the new information to your particular needs. No wonder people feel frustrated and blame themselves or the advice when they get stuck and feel like they don't know how to continue.

Self-help books and tapes often offer very little troubleshooting advice in regards to their own advice. This is like trying to install new software in a computer that is already full of old programs. If you don't take into account what is already there, the computer is likely to crash. As a result, the program does not work as promised. But it is not the software itself that is faulty; after all, it has been tested and it works on other computers. The real problem is that there are already other programs installed in the computer. If you could simply use the new program and nothing else, things would go without any problems, but of course this never happens in real life! Similarly, the most brilliant ten-step strategy will grind to halt when you do not know how to integrate it into your existing situation. Unfortunately, the how-to books rarely take this into account and rarely give you advice on how to deal with common situations like these.

How to learn, how to integrate your new knowledge into the old and how to put it into action are things that must be learned before you set out to use the how-to advice to achieve something new. Not only that, you also need to know how to avoid the common pitfalls, how to make the changes last and how to recognize if something is really working or not.

Mastering these skills is not a trick you can learn at the snap of your fingers. It takes some time and effort to learn, but it is not overly complicated and the time you invest will be well worth it. When you learn how to best use how-to and self-help resources and then put what you've learned into action, you will succeed in whatever you set out to achieve. When you add that missing "how to" to your how-to, you will be able to make that change, learn that skill or start incorporating that new habit into your life!

## Mary Looks for a Soul Mate:
## An Example of What Goes Wrong with Self-Help Advice

Mary was a career-oriented and successful woman in her mid-thirties. Earlier in her life she had dismissed finding a partner and building a relationship as something she did not have time for in her busy life. Perhaps she had also hoped that somebody would just materialize in her life by chance. But as time went by, Mary realized that she was missing something and she felt increasingly lonely. One day while browsing through a bookstore, she saw a book by a famous relationship expert and felt that it spoke directly to her. She grabbed it and read it cover-to-cover in one weekend. Inspired by the advice, and no longer content just to sit around and wait, Mary decided to actively begin searching for her soul mate.

With the help of the book, she planned her "relationship strategy:" she began to attend events where she could meet potential partners, she changed the way she dressed and spoke in order to create the "ten ways to attract love" she had read about. She felt confident and energized at the beginning, yet the confidence began to wear away as months went by and her perfect match was nowhere to be found. Pressures at work were mounting and she had less and less time to look for a relationship. She tried to consult the book, but did not find anything wrong with what she was doing, so she bought another book, just to make sure, and resolved to use all her willpower to keep trying. She focused on her goals and tried to stay positive. However, this wasn't very helpful and although she could not pinpoint what had gone wrong, she began to think that there must be something wrong with her instead. After a few more half-hearted attempts, Mary gave up.

Mary did all the right things: she found good advice and she tried hard to implement that advice. But in the end the plan did not work out. What went wrong?

Mary encountered a number of challenges which she did not know how to handle. When the books did not provide help on how to solve these problems, she didn't know where to turn and began to blame herself. But none of this was due to Mary's own shortcomings. Nor was the advice in the books at fault since they were written by recognized experts and the advice had helped other people. Mary got caught up in a typical situation where she became excited about the self-help advice and trusted that this was all she needed to know. When things didn't quite go as promised in the book, she didn't know how to react, and the other books she bought weren't much help either.

The problems compounded as Mary subsequently just tried harder, without really understanding how to go about her search for a partner and without being able to analyze what exactly went wrong. She wondered if she was the problem or if it was the advice. Even if Mary had come to the realization that she just did not work to the best of her abilities, and thus failed, this realization would not provide her with many clues on how to improve the next time. As a result, the whole experience just made Mary frustrated and disillusioned with the idea of self-development.

What Mary didn't realize was that neither the advice nor her own effort was at fault. What was really missing in Mary's case was essential information on how to deal with the inevitable issues in personal development. For example, Mary thought her willpower was the key to success, she focused very much on the end result she wanted to achieve, and she also decided to go about her self-help program alone. In fact, none of these things could help Mary to move towards her goals.

Certainly many self-help books could tell you more about how to implement the strategies, and maybe you should adjust your expectations, too. However, playing the blame game is not going to get you anywhere. The only thing that is going to help you move ahead and make progress is learning to understand why you may have difficulty acting upon the advice you receive. When you understand how to use how-to advice in the most effective way possible, you will automatically begin to discard bad advice as well as develop your ability to more objectively determine whether there was something wrong with your own actions. You will also begin to turn away from trying to find somebody at fault and move towards more constructive grounds of discovering what you can do to improve the situation.

## Checklist: Three Things That Cause You to Fail

### Poor advice

You can be given wrong or even downright dangerous advice (such as recommending a diet which does not include all the necessary nutrients). However, it is often other factors which determine your success or failure. Be honest with yourself before you blame your failure on the advice you received. Believing that the poor advice was the only reason you did not get what you wanted just serves as an excuse, allowing you to point your finger at someone else.

### Poor effort on your part

It is true that the effort you put forth is often less than 100%. It is easy to put the blame on poor effort when the promised results don't materialize. But this can also serve as an escape hatch for the authors and speakers, who can imply that their advice is just fine – it is you who has to improve.

So, is this implying that it is never your fault if you fail? Not at all. Sometimes it is your fault, and accepting this responsibility will help you to see what it takes to succeed in a more realistic light. However, cases where the problem lies in having put forth very little effort are easy to recognize and when you are honest with yourself, you will always know if this is the case.

*Not knowing how to use how-to*

Often the biggest obstacle in getting what you want is neither bad advice nor your personal failure, but rather not knowing how to use how-to in effective way. This makes analyzing the reasons for success or failure very difficult. But when you possess effective learning strategies you will have little difficulty acting upon the advice you have received.

The next chapters discuss the common shortcomings of how-to advice and show you the strategies to deal with them. It still may not be easy to achieve what you want, but you'll understand the quickest way of getting there. Knowing what makes advice work and which self-help pitfalls to avoid gives you tremendous confidence to act constructively instead of pointing fingers or making excuses.

**8.**

# Why Goals, Planning and Hard Work Are Not Enough

When authors and speakers fail to explain self-improvement ideas thoroughly, or when we fail to listen to what they are really saying, we become stuck or stagnant in our efforts to implement the advice we get. Common misconceptions can undermine an otherwise perfectly good personal improvement effort.

For example, one of the most dangerous misconceptions you can get from self-help advice is that you should focus continuously on your goals, plan everything in detail and trust that coupled with hard work, you will reap the rewards. Goals, planning and hard work are certainly necessary, but they can also lead to a lot of frustration and wasted effort when you don't understand them correctly.

But what can go wrong with focusing on goals, you ask? Virtually every book in the field emphasizes that you must have clear, preferably written goals that illustrate what you are trying to move towards. This is very good advice in itself. You need to know what you want. Unfortunately, this and other good advice has confused countless people who have overlooked it as "obvious enough" and not really understood its true meaning.

## The Danger of Focusing on Your Goals

Where many people go wrong is that they try to do exactly that: they focus on goals. They think about their goals as often as possible. They put all their energy into being positive about reaching their goals. But focusing on goals *alone* will not help you reach them, no matter how hard you try.

Do not focus solely on your goals. Instead, focus on the *steps* that you must take in order to achieve those goals. Instead of using all your time to visualize the end result, use the majority of your time to visualize the necessary steps. See yourself in your mind's eye taking those steps confidently and successfully. This is absolutely essential. The biggest obstacle you are likely to encounter along the way is that you are unable to maintain the necessary action over time. You usually manage to take a few initial steps fairly easily but then the effort falters and you eventually stop. As you begin to painfully realize that your motivation is slipping away and that you are far from achieving what you want, focusing even more intently on your goals is of no help. If you are in this situation, vividly imagining the desired outcome in your mind will just lead to increased frustration – not increased motivation.

A surefire way to ruin your chances of improvement is to focus on improvement only. Spending your time thinking about the end result will automatically lead to comparing your present situation to the ideal outcome. Instead of getting a dose of motivation, you begin to wonder if you are on the right track, you try to find signs of improvement, and you begin to avoid mistakes – after all, your vivid imagination has made sure that there is a lot at stake as far as success is concerned!

Not only that, pure goal orientation may foster the idea that you need to get this or that in order to prove to yourself that you are good or worthy. When your self-approval is only derived from *achieving* certain objectives rather than *making progress* towards them, you will be unhappy most of the time because it usually takes a while to reach anything of value.

It is more important to focus on the steps you need to take. Put your energy and imagination into making sure that you take action every day. Imagine yourself taking the steps more than you imagine yourself rising to the prizewinner's podium at the end of it all. This will take the weight of the larger goals off your shoulders. Ask yourself this: What is going to bring me to my goal of getting into shape faster – imagining being in shape and enjoying the visualization of that result, or imagining exercising three days per week and enjoying the exercise itself?

When you learn to find enjoyment in the action itself, you will find that the results themselves also seem to come easier and faster. When you willingly take the steps, day after day, the desired outcome is virtually guaranteed to follow.

Additionally, many goals are not about *getting* things; they are about *being* something as a person. You are something by doing it on a continual basis. This suggests yet another reason why focusing on the steps themselves becomes the key to success when you want to become something. Forcing yourself to go running three times a week may get you into great shape, but if you get no pleasure and see no value in running itself and find no satisfaction in *being* a runner, then it is likely that you will eventually give up this habit, losing all the benefits.

## What Is Even More Important Than Goals

In self-development, understanding what it means to *become something* should be even more important to you than your goals themselves. This is more important because it will make it possible for you to get virtually anything you want. If you wish, you can view "becoming something" as a certain type of goal in itself. Call it whatever you'd like – the important thing is to understand the distinction. When you can make this distinction, any goal-setting exercise you see in how-to books becomes much more powerful.

Here is how to make sense of it. You normally think of goals as something you want to get. You want to "get" a relationship, a promotion, a new car, an exotic vacation, or more money in your bank account. Maybe you want everything on that list! But what you also want is *to be something* and *to feel something*. You want joy, happiness, inner peace or excitement. You want to be in great shape and healthy, you want to be a successful sales-person or you want to be happily married.

However, you cannot just "get" a happy marriage, you have to "be" happily married. Being something or feeling something is not something that you can just get once and then have for the rest of your life. You can get a car, house or money but you need to *maintain* fitness or a relationship. You maintain these things by taking care of them on a continual basis. Taking care of them means *doing*, so you come back to the point that you need to find enjoyment in the action steps themselves, not just in the results.

When you really learn that you have the following two types

of objectives in your life – getting things and becoming something – you begin to make faster progress towards them than if you simply treated all your goals alike. The process of getting something can be very different from becoming something. In fact, you often need to become something before you can get something else. For example, to earn a degree, you have to become a student and a smart worker. In order to rebuild a marriage, you have to become a better partner and lover.

Interestingly, in order to have anything, you probably need to possess some skills, habits and abilities, in other words, *be* something. In order to have a happy marriage and kids (meaning: to *be* happily married), you need to *become* a lot of things. Trivial as it may sound, you first need to become an independent adult, a process that can take awhile. Then you need to become sufficiently sociable and nice so that you can attract another independent person. This also may take awhile. Normally, you then go through the phases of becoming friends, lovers and partners for life. All along the way, you do things to maintain and develop the relationship. After you eventually get married, you have to go on maintaining the marriage; then you have children, you become a parent and raise them.

See? There is no way you can just "get" a happy marriage and kids, you have to become a lot of things beforehand, and when you have achieved this, you still have to maintain it every day. Luckily, everything that you did along the way was fun in itself, and when you look back, you are most likely to say that the journey was absolutely necessary in order to really enjoy, appreciate and feel that you've earned the end result of it all: being happily married with kids. And when you are finally there, you realize that it is actually daily life itself (in other words, being) that is the most important and joyful thing.

So the next time you set goals, remember that not all goals are created alike. Understand these distinctions and you'll have a much easier time creating a plan which will get you to your destination. You will also understand why you sometimes need to take the time to build a strong foundation first before you can get what you want.

## The Danger of Planning

How to put all the self-help advice into practice? How-to books usually offer the classical three-step-model:

1. Analyze the situation and *plan* what you will do.
2. Take *action* according to your plan.
3. *Adjust* your plan and actions according to the feedback.

After the author has given some background theory about human achievement, you are supposed to make a plan, then take action, and adjust your behavior as you go along. This model is so simple that it can be, and has been, applied to virtually anything you want to do. Unfortunately, there is a slight problem. It often fails to work.

The problem is that most people's minds have already wandered off halfway through all the theoretical explanations and planning stages and they are not coming back. Often the "theory" is not really needed at all. You already know what you should do (we're often smarter than we think), yet you are frustrated because you cannot bring yourself to do what you already know. When this is combined with starting every self-help effort with arduous planning where you must figure out what you want in life, what your identity is, what your values are and so on, no wonder you get stuck and never manage to take action! Or if you do get moving, you don't know how to keep going for any meaningful period of time.

## Two Critical Mistakes in Planning

There are two critical mistakes that you can make when following any self-improvement program:

- Too much planning and information gathering in the beginning stages – leading to the postponement of action and then the slow development of turning these actions into habits.
- Too little emphasis on how to keep up your new activities – leading to the abandonment of effort after the first excitement wears off.

It is not the fault of self-help authors that they invariably begin with long explanations and planning before they get to the action part. The book format naturally lends itself to this kind of organization. It would be very difficult for any author to convince you on the first page to put the book down and take immediate, concrete action. You would simply skip this altogether and continue reading. It is far easier to follow this procedure at a live workshop, where the trainer can get everyone to perform a certain exercise or participate in an activity right at the beginning. However, don't let the standard format of how-to books fool you. Begin by taking action immediately; don't wait until you have read the whole book.

Once you get moving, plan that you will never stop. Most efforts don't fail in the beginning; they fail in the *middle* when you are unable to keep going. Any smoker can quit for a couple of days or a week, but most will start again because they do not know how to keep up the necessary effort. The same thing – abandoning your efforts after a short period of time – will happen in any personal development attempt if you do not employ the right strategies. Use your planning time to figure out *how you can continuously keep taking action in the right direction*, then follow these actions to their completion, and your life will never be the same again.

## The Alternative Success Formula

You usually don't fail because of insufficient planning or not enough knowledge. The biggest challenge is getting yourself to take forceful action, and then keeping that action going for a prolonged period of time. To do that, you need to slightly modify the classical three-step approach and make it look like this:

1. Take *action* in the right direction
   (you'll have a rough idea where).
2. Take more *action* just to reinforce this habit (just do it).
3. *Plan* what you are going to do and who is going to help you.
4. Take *action* again (now according to your plan).
5. *Adjust* your plan and actions according to the feedback.

If you plan *after* having already taken some action, you have just demonstrated to yourself that you can get things done. You have gained momentum and it is easier to believe that you will turn your plan into reality.

This is how it would work if you decided to lose weight, for example:

1. Go for a short walk or jog. Now.
2. Do it again tomorrow. Feel the energy and the satisfaction you get from taking action.
3. Only *after* these initial action steps move on to planning your weight loss program and reading those diet books. Try to involve a friend to support you.
4. Take action again and feel how you are already on your way to creating an action habit.
5. Adjust your actions according to feedback.

You need some faith to get started. You'll never have all the answers when you are starting out and it's impossible to create the perfect plan. The best way to get some faith is to do something – anything – and think on your feet. Take the risk of action. It is much smaller than the risk of not taking any action at all. Action will give you a tremendous surge of motivation because you move from the realm of a purely intellectual exercise (thinking and planning) into something that rewards you with immediate physical feelings and energy.

### Create an Action Habit

Getting started is actually much less energy consuming than planning and procrastinating. You'll find that you are more energized *after* doing something than before you begin. This works not only in the beginning, but also when you stagnate in your efforts. When your energy or conviction begins to falter, the natural tendency is to stop "to rest and gather more strength." Often, this will only make you lose your momentum, not help you to get back on track. Action is what keeps you energetic, both physically and mentally. The fastest way to improve your life is to create an action habit:

- Do something now. Don't postpone it until tomorrow.
- If you do not know what to do, just do *something*!
- Get physical. Physical and mental energies are connected.
- Just do it. You can't fail as badly doing something as you could fail doing nothing.

When you want to improve your life it does not matter that you are *capable* of doing things, or that you *know* a lot about things. The only thing that matters is *will* you do something? *Will* you take action? *Will* you keep going day after day?

You do need to make sure that you are taking intelligent action, but far more personal development endeavors have failed because of a lack of action rather than for the lack of knowledge. However, action orientation does not mean filling up your calendar with hundreds of things to do and then becoming terribly busy. Quite the contrary, it means reflecting upon whether you are doing the right kinds of things and making sure that you can continue doing what really matters.

## Why Getting Real Results Takes Time and Effort: The S-Curve Explained

If you have been wondering why – despite all the great advice you have received – some self-improvement results are slower to observe than others, the so-called *S-curve* will help you to understand why this is so. When you see how it applies to self-development advice, it is suddenly clear why tremendous improvements rarely occur within a few days, but also why you can sometimes make such fast progress that it is nothing short of a miracle. The S-curve can be your ally when you come to understand it or it can be your enemy if you fail to grasp its meaning. This is what the S-curve looks like:

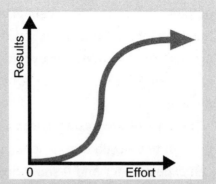

What the S-curve illustrates is very simple: At the beginning, you have to exert a great deal of effort to get moving, yet you will get relatively few results in return for this effort. Once you get moving, it becomes easier and easier, and the rewards for your effort increase quickly. But at some point, the rewards begin to diminish again and you have to work harder and harder for even small gains.

An example of this would be learning a foreign language. You first struggle to understand the structure, the grammar and the vocabulary, but as you get past this first stage, you find yourself making very fast progress. However, at some point you will reach a plateau where your efforts produce less noticeable results, even if you spend a lot of time practicing your language skills.

Another example is changing your habits. You must first exert a great deal of effort to make even small gains, and everything will seem difficult (the beginning of S-curve), but if you keep at it, you'll find that the going gets easier and you'll start to see great results (the middle of S-curve). However, trying to create the kind of unrealistic habits that will not let you slip up one single time for the rest of your life (the end of S-curve), will require tremendous effort and is not likely to bring much good anyway.

In fact, the S-curve affects everything we do. Sometimes it is steeper, sometimes it is flatter, but the principle stays the same. It depicts the ratio of "effort versus results." It shows you that nothing comes for free, especially in the beginning, and that reaching for absolute perfection is going to cost an overwhelming amount of resources for ever decreasing gains. The S-curve can be divided into the parts of increasing returns and diminishing returns

The part of *increasing returns* occurs after you have broken through the inertia that is keeping things the way they are. You can expect faster and faster gains as the gains you have made

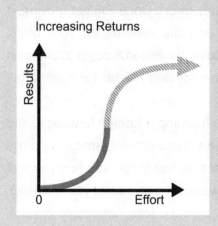

build upon each other. In other words, your self-improvement efforts will require the most effort at the beginning and get progressively easier as you learn and practice more.

The part of *diminishing returns* occurs when the quick gains are slowing down and each amount of effort you put forth results in smaller and smaller improvements. In time, when you get very proficient at something, the more work you put in towards the task of getting even better at what you are doing, the less you will get in return.

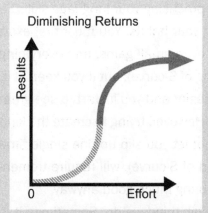

This does not mean that you should not bother improving yourself, just that you need to be aware of when you have gained enough and then move on to new, complementary areas. When you read books on sales techniques, for example, and you really make an effort to learn something, the first 10 books will raise you to a completely new level of sales success. The next 10 or 20 will be useful as well, but after that you are learning less and less for all the time you spend. The smart thing to do is not to stop reading, but to change subjects. Select several books on self-motivation and you'll not only lear quickly again, but you'll also find ideas that will greatly contribute to your sales success.

Because you and the world around you keep changing, you cannot view progress in any one area as a single S-curve; often improvement consists of a series of S-curves. Progress and improvement are not linear.

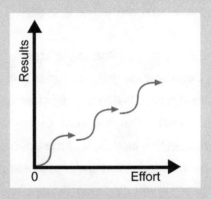

As you progress, you may actually go backwards for a short time before you return to the new growth curve. This can be compared to a child who has learned to crawl on all fours and who can move relatively quickly, yet she is now learning to walk, a process which makes her movements initially very slow but will ultimately allow her to run faster than she could ever crawl. Similarly, when Tiger Woods decided to change his mechanics of hitting a golf ball, his performance initially suffered a setback, but after getting the hang of it, his new style allowed him to hit better than ever before.

The S-curve can help you to understand the following points:

- You must pay the price to reap the rewards. Nothing comes without effort, but once you get moving, even making a small effort can bring big rewards.
- Focus on the things that really matter, and you will reap disproportionate rewards. Search for absolute perfection in one area, and your time will be spent on matters of ever-decreasing importance.
- Your progress will rarely be linear; it will accelerate and decelerate.
- In order to move to a higher level of performance, you should be prepared for a small setback before you become proficient in your new way of doing things.

### The 80/20 rule and the S-Curve

Understanding the S-curve will also give you deeper insights into the 80/20 rule which is frequently used in how-to books. You remember that the rule simply states that 80% of the value results from only 20% of the actions. The usual conclusion is that you should concentrate your efforts only on those actions that will bring you disproportionate rewards, all the rest is unproductive use of your time. However, this only works when we can freely choose where we concentrate our efforts. Self-help books and trainers give great advice on what to do, providing a guideline for what works. If you will, this is like pointing towards the middle part of the S-curve and telling you that putting your efforts into these specific actions will bring you bigger rewards than anything else you can do.

However, it is clear that particularly in the short term, you are not always free to choose where you can put all your efforts. To reap the rewards of focusing your actions according to the 80/20 principle, you often have to prepare a little. You can't always skip the beginning of the S-curve where the gains come slowly. Even when you implement advice immediately, it will require some time before you begin to feel the effects even.

Why does this matter? It matters because it has made countless people confused about the advice they get from well-meaning self-help trainers. Even extremely powerful principles that are absolutely guaranteed to work, even when applied immediately, are not going to change your life in a day. You can make immediate changes to your attitude, your feelings, your inner motivation, but to apply those changes to a real-life situation will take some time. First, if you are beginning a new activity, you need time to learn; you cannot jump straight into being proficient and effective. Second, if you are trying to change old actions or habits, you still need some time to organize and communicate to yourself and others how it is going to be from now on. You are not going to feel that you are getting 80% of the results for just 20% of the work. In fact, at the beginning you may feel that nothing much has changed at all.

The key is not to become disillusioned by the advice and not to start thinking that those life-changing principles were not all they cracked up to be, but rather to work through the beginning of the S-curve first. Only then will you fully begin to realize the promised benefits. No matter how powerful the principle is that you are applying, you need to give it some time to work its magic, in which case it is necessary to look beyond the slow start of the S-curve and keep believing you'll eventually see results.

# 9.

# Why Knowledge Does Not Equal Learning

This chapter is about learning, but it is not about how to learn to read faster, how to process a lot of information or how to develop a superb memory. These things are useful but not really important. What is really important is to understand that the way you define learning determines your potential to improve your life and to develop as a human being.

What does this really mean? It simply means that if you are attached to the old notion that learning is synonymous with gathering knowledge, you will never achieve your full potential no matter how hard you try. To get the most out of self-help advice you must redefine what learning means to you.

One of the hardest things about self-development is to admit that knowledge does not necessarily equal learning, and that you cannot expect results just by absorbing more information. We fool ourselves all the time by going to a bookstore, buying a self-help book, and then patting ourselves on the back for having taken the first step towards what we want to achieve. We get instant satisfaction from buying that book, we even begin to read it and nod our head in agreement with all the good points, but too often this is as far as we go. We never take any consistent action based on our new knowledge. Not only that, we actually tell ourselves that some day, now that we know what we should do, we are going to make the effort. Of course, this rarely happens.

## The Knowledge Myth

The problem is this: somewhere, somehow, you got the idea into your head that when you know *about* something, you have learned it. Unfortunately, this is not enough.

There are many business school students who upon graduation know a considerable amount about "management." They have studied it for years. Yet these graduates are never immediately given the position as the manager of a company. Why? Because although they may *know* a great deal, they have not actually *done* anything. There is a big difference between knowing something and actually doing it on a consistent basis. In addition, there is also quite a bit of knowledge that you can only acquire and maintain through practical experience.

Being clever and knowledgeable about something gives us satisfaction. And it is often very easy to derive this sort of satisfaction – just open up a newspaper and you already "know" more than you did five minutes earlier. However, there is still a long way to go from storing this information to actually *being able to use it*, and finally, to actually *putting it to use*.

Being exposed to information is not really learning. You have learned almost nothing by just learning about something. Modern definitions of learning state that if there is no change in your behavior (or your thought processes and the output thereof), then no real learning has taken place.

What you have learned up until this point of the book or what you have learned throughout your life is of little value if you do not put it to use. In fact, we could claim that before you actually put your knowledge to use, you have not really learned it at all. No amount of knowledge *about* exercise will get you into shape; only exercise on a regular basis will.

What you want to learn from how-to and self-help books has very little to do with "knowing." It has more to do with acquiring an ability to do something and then *doing it* – day in, day out.

Learning about things has its place and you *do* need to gather knowledge. But self-development is not just an intellectual exercise – it is about learning to put something into practice and about making very real changes in your life. It is about taking action and creating new habits.

If you want to get the most out of your personal improvement efforts, whether it be with the help of a book, video or a workshop, from now on define learning as a change in your physical and mental behavior. For your purposes, any other kind of learning will not help you make progress.

## How Much Information Do You Need?

**Q:** *What Does Quantum Physics Have to Do with Riding a Bicycle?*

**A:** Nothing at all, actually. Quantum physics has nothing to do with our ability to ride a bicycle, yet that is exactly where many of us try to begin when we want to learn something new.

Remember when you learned to ride a bicycle? Ask yourself this: Did someone explain beforehand the biomechanics and the physics involved? No, of course not. And if they had, would you have learned to ride a bike any faster? No, of course not! Learning to ride a bike is something that can only be done through practice, by summoning up your courage and giving it a go.

Yet this is rarely the way we adults approach learning something new. Instead of practicing, we begin by gathering all kinds of information that most probably in the end will just serve to slow down our learning, not make it any faster. Not only do we want information, but we want the latest and the best – we want scientific theory, research data, the latest studies and consultants' recommendations. Perversely, we often want to believe that anything worthwhile must be complex.

We are so conditioned to think about learning as "learning about" instead of "learning to be" and "learning to do" that we have lost our ability to take meaningful action. Riding a bicycle can be broken down into the most complex scientific explanation imaginable – ranging from thousands of bodily functions to the mechanics of the bike in movement to the friction of the tire on the road. But knowing about all this won't help you ride any better.

Not only do we waste time by gathering information that won't help (but which offers us a quick fix by fooling us into thinking that we have actually learned something), we may even feel a little threatened by the fact that a child can learn to ride a bicycle faster than we can despite all of our superior knowledge. We may feel threatened by the fact that something as simple as the common self-help principles could have a big impact in our lives, and we outright refuse to believe other people who claim to have done it. It upsets our belief system which maintains that we can only get ahead with superior intelligence and knowledge.

In fact, all the thinking, analyzing and "Quantum physics" only takes time away from real learning. Whether it is personal development or learning how to ride a bike, only practice is going to create results.

**Q:** *What Does Newtonian Physics Have to Do with Self-Help?*
**A:** Surprisingly, quite a lot. Consider the following: You were probably taught so-called Newtonian physics at school. You learned about a man named Isaac Newton who, according to the story, discovered the principle of gravity by observing an apple drop to the ground. You learned about the laws which govern the movement of bodies in time and space. You learned about gravity and friction and why the planets keep circling the sun. Yet the reality is that for the past one hundred years, Newtonian physics has no longer been considered by scientists to accurately describe the world in which we live. Already in the first half of the last century, Quantum physics began to replace the Newtonian view of the world and it has been for decades what all universities teach to freshman classes of physics students.

So why were you still taught Newtonian physics at school? The reason is that Quantum physics is a very complex science and requires a lot of study in order to be understood. Newtonian physics, on the other hand, is easy to understand and it *approximates* reality close enough to be useful. While it is not a completely accurate representation of how scientists believe our world to function, it is so close that it is useful. You can use Newtonian physics to understand how the world works and easily apply what you have learned. While quantum theory would be even more accurate, this comes at a greatly increased cost in learning time and is usually not worth the effort for a normal person.

So what has this got to do with personal development? It turns out that much what the how-to and self-help authors and speakers tell you is also only an adequate approximation of how things work. It is not the absolutely all-encompassing model which includes the latest scientific research. Nor does it have to be, because it is a close enough model to be both understandable and useful to you. This is what matters. For most of us, most of the time, a good approximation that we can understand is enough because learning every last detail is not likely to be worth the effort.

A scientist may be able to point out an exception to the rule or the principle you learned from how-to or self-help books, but if the model itself works well, this probably does not matter a great deal. This is especially true in the field of human achievement where we cannot measure with mathematical perfection certain factors such as life's purpose, feelings, attitudes or beliefs.

## Acquire the Fundamentals

You will be doing yourself a big favor if you take some time to think about all the "success principles" that you already know. Are you one of the many people who thinks that they have already heard all these principles? Or are you one of the few people who has actually learned them?

Consider goal setting, a basic skill promoted by every self-help coach. The simple idea is that if you don't know your destination, you will have hard time getting there. Guess how many people who have learned *about* goal setting are actually putting it into practice so that their daily life reflects their objectives? That's right – only very few. There is nothing demanding about it, certainly nothing secret about it, yet most people still fail to do it. People dismiss the idea, presumably because they feel that they already know everything, and then they move on to the next idea. Not only that, people are disdainful towards the trainers who present these "too basic" ideas; they want to move on to the "advanced stuff." However, if we use the definition of learning as a change in behavior, these people have rarely even learned the basics.

You can read an entire book in this way, understanding what it says but failing to get a single benefit out of it for your life. And you may never even realize it, congratulating yourself for being one smart cookie – you've already read five books this month! When a book promises to teach you everything you need to know about personal success, the promise is easily kept. Unfortunately, that doesn't do anything for you. Nobody can pour something into your head and make things happen effortlessly. You need to make an effort to really learn something and practice what you have learned.

The fundamentals are often not mind-blowing concepts, but if you learn them and practice them, they can yield absolutely mind-blowing results. Don't dismiss learning something because it seems so obvious – the most powerful ideas often are. Acquire the fundamentals but accept that it will take some time and effort to do so.

> *"If calculus were invented today, none of our corporations*
> *could learn it. We'd send everyone off to the three day*
> *course...give them three months to try it out and see if 'it*
> *worked'. After it had failed, we'd conclude that it was of*
> *little value and move to something else."*
>     – An anonymous manager from Ford, quoted by
>       Peter Senge in his book *The Fifth Discipline*

Your mind needs to process things and get feedback from your actions in order for real learning to take place. There are no shortcuts you can take in order to achieve something really valuable in your life. This isn't saying that it is complicated (it isn't) or that it takes years (it doesn't). But everything has just changed because you are dealing with a new definition of learning and you can't fool yourself anymore. Maybe it is now easier to also understand why there can be too much good advice in the average how-to or self-help book. Some are such treasures that if you were to put all that advice into action as you were reading it, it would take you several months or even a year to go through the contents of this single book. Of course, we are often too tempted to move faster, and therefore, we may skip many of the useful learning opportunities that are right under our noses.

## Learn the Important Things, Not Everything

Learning comes at a cost. The cost is your time and effort, both of which you have a limited amount. Learning *about* things can be done easily and almost endlessly. Real learning, the kind where you change your behavior and master something new, is much more energy and time consuming. Learning will in turn create new energy and motivation, but the time is something that you will never be able to get back.

You simply cannot afford to learn everything. Painstakingly learning all the fine details will make you an expert on the subject matter at hand, but will leave you with little time for anything else. Therefore, instead of learning everything, learn the key things. Instead of looking for a perfect but very complex model of the world (Quantum physics), look for an understandable approximation first (Newtonian physics).

What you read in the how-to and self-help books is rarely the whole story. It is simplified, intensified and pruned clear of exceptions or contradictions. But when the authors and speakers get it right, it will be the 20% of the story that accounts for 80% of the results, and that is ultimately what matters to you. You need to discover which ideas have the biggest impact on your life and what would help you the most to reach your goals. You will virtually always find that this is also the case – although there may be hundreds of factors affecting an outcome, only a few key actions have the biggest impact and bring the majority of results. This effect has been observed to work in all walks of life from movie production (big hits bring in all the revenues) to improving your health (eliminating a small minority of foodstuffs that are the most detrimental to your health reaps big rewards), and the same principle will work in your personal development efforts as well.

Your life is too short to learn everything indiscriminately. Use experts who have already succeeded in discovering the important leverage points and concentrate your learning efforts on them.

## Forming Patterns in Your Mind and Body

When you learn, you create patterns in your mind and body. The brain forms new connections and neural pathways that allow you to perform tasks. Your body does the same in connection with the brain by storing information in the neuromuscular memory which then allows you to recall and perform movements and other bodily functions accurately.

This can be compared to a set of paths in the forest (in fact, there are physical pathways in your brain between the neurons). It is most efficient to follow the well-established tracks which in turn become even more established the more you use them. With some effort, it is possible to go anywhere in the forest, totally off the beaten track. But unless you follow this new pathway repeatedly, thus creating a new path altogether, it is always going to be strenuous exercise. Learning new things is like forming a new path, requiring some effort at first, but then it gets progressively easier the more you do it. However, without repeated exercise (following your new path), the effects will be minimal. In addition, the old paths need to be maintained. Once you have it, you need to use it or lose it. The paths start to fade away if they are not used, which of course can also be a good thing if you are trying to forget your old ways. Maintaining well-traveled paths is easy – they are already so established that for them to disappear, you need to be neglectful of them for a long time.

Of course, the more paths you have formed, the easier and quicker it is to use them to get anywhere you want. It is also increasingly easy to lay down new tracks because there are already so many that they can be connected with.

On a path you know well, you can let your subconscious autopilot guide you, hardly expending any mental energy on the task.

This is what many of us experience when driving a car; we do not have to think about it at all. When you are learning something new, like when you learn to drive for the first time, you have to use all your mental energy to complete the task. This is why learning about what you already know comes easily (you are using well-established paths), and it is also why completely changing the way you think requires a lot of effort (you are going off the beaten track). The paths you create, whether on purpose or involuntarily, form a pattern of thinking, doing and feeling which guides your life. You cannot learn to ride a bike by reading a manual because you need to form the necessary patterns in your mind and this can happen only through practice. Sometimes you can form new patterns in an instant, for example when you have a very strong emotional experience. Often it takes months of practice to master something. Even when the initial change happens very quickly, we need to practice repeatedly to refine and perfect a new pattern. To learn faster, seek help from someone who already knows what to do and who can keep you moving in the right direction.

Learning is about creating patterns and that is the essence of all self-development. It is about forming new (or strengthening the existing) patterns in our brain and the body, finding help from the authors and trainers who can coach us, and making sure we are doing the right things. Then we have to practice until we have mastered the task and have made it an established part of what we are; that is, it has become a subconscious activity at the deepest level that we no longer have to think about.

# 10.

# Learning Effectively

No "success program" can do our learning for us. We need to actively use our own experiences to learn what works and what doesn't. No matter what the motivational speakers say or what you read in a how-to book, things and circumstances are going to turn out to be a little different in your own life. You will have no problem dealing with this and applying their advice to your own situation when you understand how the so-called *learning cycle* works – but you will be very confused if you don't understand this. Relying on only one formula or one guru will make you inflexible, but understanding how to experiment, improvise and apply what you learn will open unlimited possibilities.

Learning-by-doing is one of the most powerful ways of achieving the kind of life you want. When you learn from your own actions and incorporate the successful ones into your daily life as habits, your progress becomes unstoppable.

**Learning-By-Doing: The Learning Cycle**

*"One cannot teach a man anything. One can only enable him to learn from within himself."*
                                        – Galileo Galilei

Nobody has ever started out as an instant expert or has gone straight to success. These are things individuals have had to learn how to do. Some people learned faster, some slower, but they all learned by going through the learning cycle, also known as the *feedback loop*, over and over again. The idea is simple: You set out to do something, you do it, and then evaluate what happened. Based on the evaluation, you then do it again and again, adjusting your behavior until you have mastered it. You may not get the desired outcome the first time, or even the tenth time, but if you keep on correcting your actions according to the feedback, you will eventually get there.

Feedback loops steer our actions from mundane everyday things like opening a lock with your key (based on the feedback from your eyes and hands, your brain guides your hand to fit the key into the lock) to major efforts like earning a university degree (the feedback from the teachers guides you towards completing all the necessary requirements).

The principle of learning-by-doing is illustrated by the picture of the feedback loop. The learning cycle consists of interplay between *action* and *reflection* (the big circle in the illustration). During the particular action, the feedback is usually immediate and you adjust your approach as you go along (the smaller circle in the illustration). To make sense of it all, however, you need to pause and reflect. When you reflect upon the feedback in your

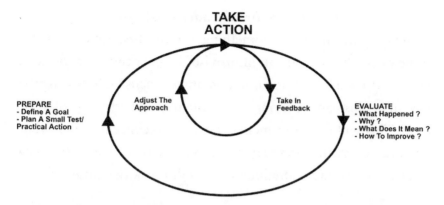

mind and make meaning of the outcome, you begin to develop new understanding and knowledge. This learning will then be reflected in your behavior.

The same approach works for any area of how-to or self-help that you are interested in. When you really want to learn something, you have to combine action with reflection. You cannot improve your life by just gathering information and never taking any action, nor can you improve it if all you do is take action without ever pausing to make sense of it all.

## How to Make Learning-By-Doing Effective

*Trying too hard will just interfere*

This is the time not to be too aware of everything that happens. Do not think about whether you are performing poorly or well. Let your actions flow naturally. Hold the conversation in your head to a minimum, relax and just do it. Picture yourself as a child who falls down but who just gets up and tries again. There is an effortlessness that comes from suppressing judgment, from simply observing and trusting the brain's natural ability to guide you in the right direction. The time for evaluation and analysis comes later.

### Let the step-by-step advice help you

When you are doing something for the first time, find out some of the rules. You can improvise the next time but for now, use a step-by-step plan to your advantage. Focus on following the key steps, instead of trying to invent them off the top of your head. This will free your mental capacity to concentrate on what you are doing. But don't try to keep more than one or two key ideas in your mind – anything more will break the natural flow.

### Go for the early wins

Design your actions in a such way that you can get little things accomplished in no time at all. Give yourself a chance to get encouraging feedback as early as possible; otherwise you will run out of energy and motivation.

### Always err on the side of action

If you don't know what to do, just do something! This will generate feedback and help you find the right track. And because learning is not just an intellectual exercise, but action, you must use your whole body to learn. You will discover that you do not only remember and store things in your mind, but in your body as well.

### Get immediate feedback

For learning to be most effective, the feedback must be immediate. In fact, it does not matter so much whether the feedback is positive or negative. What matters most is the time it takes for feedback to reach you. The longer it takes, the less you benefit from it.

*Stop to evaluate*

After taking action, stop for a moment to think about what you've done, what happened and what you should do next. Focus on a few key reviewing/measuring criteria: 2 to 5 is good, anything more is unnecessary. The interpretation of the outcome has a lot of power to be both good and bad. Understand that feedback is not about your worth as a human being – it is just a little experiment you've tried to do. Treat the feedback as objectively as possible and do not attach your self-worth to it. Remember, it's not Judgment Day – it's a day for learning and reflection. Don't get consumed by analyzing every aspect of your life. Make a quick mental note of the outcome and move on.

*From time to time, evaluate your values*

Before the learning cycle even begins, your values and beliefs set the stage for you. You tend to gravitate towards decisions and actions that are in sync with your values. Be aware of your values because they will make you try certain things and discard others without any conscious thought or understanding of why this may be so.

## Learning by Modelling

Life is too short to learn everything on your own by trial and error. To be an effective learner, you need to learn by modeling other people's behavior and actions. In effect, you are learning from other people's feedback loops (experience). Closely observe other people's actions and results. If you don't take advantage of learning from others, you will end up wasting a great deal of time reinventing the wheel. Others have already gone through similar situations and experiences before you. They have already learned the hard way and have discovered the little things that make a big difference. Trying to learn everything firsthand is not very resourceful. Go to those who already know.

Methods range from simple observation to the very detailed practice of NLP (Neurolinguistic Programming). Learning to emulate others is one of the key skills that you should consider acquiring. In fact, the whole self-help industry is created on the principle that if you model yourself after the experts in any given field, that is, copy their methods, you start to get similar results.

You can model yourself after a great salesperson, a happy couple, a good driver, a top athlete, or whatever else it is that you would like to become. Model yourself not only after what people do but also how they do it. How we go about something is not only about our actions but also about our thoughts, state of mind and physiology. Once you have modeled yourself after a person or a method, you can then begin to transfer what you have learned to your life. In fact, everything you do in life is based on some kind of mental model that you have learned, which guides your actions in a certain direction. Your brain is constantly filtering all the sensory information from the environment and focusing your attention only on those things that matter – and it all happens according to your mental models.

A model gives you a target to aim for, and by adjusting your actions according to the feedback you get, you can steer your way towards that target. Remember, you can't hit a target you don't see. It is very difficult to improve if you cannot compare the results of your efforts to something that represents an ideal out-come.

Out of necessity, a model must be a simplification. You can never "copy" another person exactly. A model is an approximation of reality, emphasizing certain features and letting others fade into the background. This is what we protest against when we feel that the "seven success steps" or "the five laws of personal achievement" are too simple compared to real life. They are simplified because they have to be that way. Without simplifying and bringing the essential elements to the foreground, it would be too arduous a task to be able to focus on what really matters. Model other people and use the models in how-to books to turn your attention to the right things, but remember that it is your task to form the link between the simplified representation and the real world.

It is not enough to model other people. We need to be able to model ourselves as well. Surprisingly, few people are aware of how they behave, not to mention knowing how to put themselves in the optimum state of performance at will. Becoming more aware of how we are doing things is often a more profound learning experience than simply emulating others. Copying others is only going to take us so far if we are not really familiar with the structure (ourselves) to which we are trying to attach these new ways of doing things.

## Your Challenge: Finding Cause and Effect

One of your challenges in personal development will be making sure that you are paying enough attention to cause and effect. Most of the time – if you think about it – the connection between cause and effect is easy to see. You understand that whatever you do, or whatever you leave undone, is going to have some effect on your life. But sometimes you do not recognize the effect at all, thus making it hard to steer your actions. There are three issues you need to contend with:

### Connect cause and effect

Most people fail to introduce deliberate cause and effect thinking into their daily habits and actions. Consider this example: If you have decided to take up jogging and then abandon this new habit for a couple of days, you'll probably just shrug your shoulders and not give it much thought. If this is the case, you probably haven't attached any real consequences to not jogging. If you don't introduce immediate effects, such as some type of reward or "punishment" (just a call from your friend will suffice, there's no need to become too grim!), it is no wonder your best intentions are slipping through your fingers. Become more aware of cause and effect. Your plans and promises need to have real and tangible consequences. And the more immediate the feedback, the easier it is to steer yourself in the right direction.

### Dig deeper to find the real effect

When you are dealing with complex systems and interactions between people, cause and effect can feel disconnected. When you do something (cause), the results (effect) may happen somewhere else in time and space. Consider this example: If you are an assistant manager and you fail to complete a task on time, therefore passing it down the line too late, someone else will suffer. If the organization is hierarchical, you may never even hear about this directly, and the only time you'll feel the effects of what you started is when somebody down the line suddenly becomes unwilling to work with you anymore. If you've never stopped to consider the relationship between your actions and the resulting effect, all of this remains a mystery to you. Remember, there is a cause for every effect, even when the relationship or connection between them is not so easily discerned.

### Understand that effects accumulate

Many effects only accumulate over time, making it harder to recognize their cause. There may be no immediate consequences for your action or non-action. Consider a person who neglects higher education. For the first years following school, he or she could be doing fine and there is probably little difference between this individual and the others in the same age group. But as the years go by, that person finds it harder and harder to get promoted to well-paying jobs, while those who have the educational background start to get ahead. The immediate consequence of not getting an education is not that significant, but the long-term effect on one's life is tremendous. Or consider driving a car. You may need your car to get to work, but at the same time driving releases pollution into the environment. Unfortunately, the effects accumulate and we are not going to see them until much later, perhaps when it is too late to do anything about it.

The biggest obstacles along your road to success are not those insurmountable difficulties which grind your progress to a halt, but rather the biggest problem is often that you do not get instant feedback on your actions, making it very hard to adjust your actions. It is difficult to improve if you don't instantly get to see whether what you did resulted in success or failure, whether it was a step in the right direction or a step backwards. As this difficulty is compounded by our busy lives where we fail to stop and reflect upon what is happening, no wonder we find it difficult to succeed.

Decide to become more aware of the causes and effects in your life. Make things matter to you. It is a prerequisite for achieving any important goal.

## Sometimes Theory Is the Most Practical Thing You Can Learn

A good theory is enormously useful. However, self-help and how-to resources routinely provide minimum theory and as many practical ways of doing things as possible. However, if you are only looking for the "practical examples" you will end up missing out on the power of a good theory. A good theory is the most practical thing you can learn. Although it may sometimes seem this way, theories were not invented to make learning seem dry and detached from the real world. Theories were invented to provide a basis for a maximum number of applications in the most compact form possible. Consider mathematical formulas, for example. They are extremely compact, yet very powerful when you know how to use them. There is nothing lifeless about a good theory: Laws of physics can be used to explain how to throw the meanest possible curve ball in the game of baseball, for example.

A theory or a model is useful because it tells you not only what works, but also why something works. You can then test and apply this in various situations. Theory allows you to experiment and then compare the results, further refining the theory, not just recording single events.

Many people say, "Don't give me all this theoretical stuff, just tell me how to put it into practice." They want to get on with the practical side of it all, which is perfectly fine in itself. But theory learning is also important and if you think that it is not for you,

you are greatly limiting your potential and actually making learning harder for yourself. One of the ironies of life is that it is exactly when you are learning-by-doing that the theory has its greatest power. When you go through the learning cycle and adjust your actions based on the feedback you get, what you are in fact doing is creating a theory in itself. The connection your mind makes between the actions you took and the outcomes that resulted can be seen as a simple theory. You can quickly test this theory by taking more action and observing the outcomes. In that sense, you are always involving a little bit of theory in your learning, whether you are aware of it or not. By all means skip the dry, unnecessarily complicated theories that are full of words you do not understand. But do not skip the power of the theory itself.

## Learning in Complex Situations:
## From Stimulus-Response to Systems Thinking

Many self-help authors use the phrase "madness is doing the same thing over and over again and expecting a different outcome." They use it to encourage you to change your approach when you are not getting the results you want. While this is very good advice, life throws some extra complexity your way. It turns out that in real life you sometimes *do* get different results from doing the same thing over and over again. How can this be?

To simplify things, how-to and self-help trainers explain their principles in terms of a stimulus-response model. If you put in a certain kind of stimulus, you will get a certain kind of response. Smile and people will be friendlier to you in return. This demonstrates simple cause and effect with almost mechanical reliability.

In comparison, *systems thinking,* a relatively recent field of study, states that many things don't obey a direct stimulus-response model. Instead, they are "living systems," behaving like organisms that evolve over time. What this means is that when you put in a stimulus, the response will not be the same every time. It changes and may produce quite unexpected results. As your stimulus (your actions) affects a complex system like a human being or an organization, it often changes the system itself, making it react differently to the same actions over time. It may also produce a change in some other connected areas, which you may or may not notice, or it may compound the effects of your actions until one day, quite suddenly, it no longer responds the way it used to. Systems thinking provides a new toolbox for understanding how to reach your objectives when this happens.

The fact is, life is both complex *and* simple. The challenge with self-development is that sometimes we can safely operate using the mechanistic view, expecting more or less the same outcome from the same action, and sometimes we need to move to systems thinking to understand what is really happening. The how-to advice you base your actions on may not always produce the kind of results you expected. The world around us keeps evolving and we must be ready to adjust to it. Anybody who has tried to using the "10 Best Closing Phrases" from a how-to sales book published in 1985 is painfully aware of this – they have literally been laughed out of the client's conference room. The system (the buyer) has changed just by having been exposed to these particular closing techniques, producing a very different response compared with when they were first introduced.

How do you deal with complex systems then? What you need to do is look beyond the simple step-by-step formulas and understand the concepts behind them: You need to look for the emerging patterns and focus on what is really happening instead of what is supposed to be happening. You need to listen to the advice of those who have been in similar situations and see if you can find comparable patterns to fit or match your own. You need to realize that cause and effect are not always closely linked and immediately recognizable. You have to dig a little deeper to see how things are interconnected. Now you get to be creative and learn something instead of trying to copy-paste a lifeless model into your life – you need to get involved.

Systems thinking is one reason why a holistic approach to self-improvement is effective. The more areas of yourself you develop, the more you become aware of how things are interconnected, the more methods or strategies you have to help you arrive at the desired outcome. The same actions may not always result in the same outcome but you have the flexibility to work with whatever happens and select a route that eventually gets you to your destination.

Many authors, even when they never mention the word systems thinking, acknowledge its effects by explaining how some things only work with time, how things are interconnected and how your actions have a compounding effect as well as a direct one. It would be tempting to say that systems thinking is somehow more advanced or the ultimate key to self-development, but it is not. It is a different way of thinking and may work well in certain cases but not so well in others. Often the "traditional" stimulus-response thinking is quicker to grasp and gives a close enough representation of how the world works. Remember, the model you are using does not have to be perfect, but it has to be close enough to produce meaningful results. Sometimes the stimulus-response model is close enough, sometimes systems thinking is more useful.

## Ideas and Innovations Often Arise from Initial Confusion

Sometimes you will not get the straightforward results you expect and you'll find it hard to understand what really happened. This can be frustrating when you have a clear goal in mind and you would like to get there as quickly as possible. But complexity has its benefits. It gives rise to combinations that otherwise would never have come up. Life frequently yields total surprises. This can provide insights that are tremendously more valuable than if the results we were expecting had just fallen into our laps. Almost all the great inventions – from antibiotics to the telephone – have resulted from something completely unexpected happening during an experiment.

> *"System power is the ability to act as if you can make happen whatever it is you want to have happen, knowing that you cannot, and being willing to live with and work with whatever does happen."*
> – Barry Oshry

Traditionally, learning-by-doing emphasizes that when we have to learn new things, we will make mistakes at first, but through practice we'll get better and better and the number of mistakes we make will eventually decrease. However, as the rate of changes in our lives picks up, and as there is ever more information available, there is no longer time to become really efficient at something just from learning-by-doing – the system keeps changing slightly all the time.

In these situations you need to learn *innovatively*. You need to grasp a concept and expand and apply it to new, different contexts – all at the same time believing that your own actions will give it direction and create something of value. Because of this, it is more important than ever to be active in your learning, not just by accumulating knowledge, but by actively shaping the system in question. As a participant in systems, you are a co-creator and by being willing to work with them, you begin to change these systems. Personal development and learning becomes "creation" and those two concepts are inseparable. In these situations, learning-by-doing takes on a whole new meaning: you are not just learning about the world, you are actively shaping it as well.

# Avoiding the Self-Help Pitfalls

In addition to the information that you are interested in learning, self-help and how-to books also contain things that you would be better off without. No, self-improvement is not dangerous; there is no subliminal "black magic" that you can inadvertently pick up somewhere between the lines which will mess up your life. But there are very real ways of misusing a good thing. By not paying attention to what you are doing, you can fall into one of the common pitfalls that awaits you when you try to improve your life.

Think about jogging for example. Everybody agrees that it is good for you (even those who have never tried it). But jogging, as simple an activity as it is, can also be done incorrectly. You are not doing yourself any good if you jog too much, if you jog too little, or if you jog against the doctor's orders. Jogging is not good for you when you jog on a hard surface or immediately after eating; jogging is dangerous when it's too hot outside and jogging without good shoes can cause serious physical problems. None of these things is likely to destroy your health completely, but they certainly do not improve it either and make all that jogging a wasted effort.

There are similar ways you can waste a lot of time and effort on self-help and how-to by picking up negative influences or habits. This chapter will explain how to avoid the most common self-improvement pitfalls and keep a good thing a good thing.

## The Uniqueness Error

*"I am so unique / my situation is so unique that it's no wonder the usual advice does not work for me. I have to keep searching for something that is exactly right for me..."*

Many authors and speakers *do* say that everyone on Earth is a unique individual who has the capability of living their life in a way no other human can. This is true – you are unique. But on the other hand, it is also true that you're not unique at all. You are like thousands or even millions of people before you who have been in similar situations in their lives.

Sound harsh? It is not – it is actually very liberating. It liberates you from the excuse that so far nothing has worked for you because your situation is so unique. It liberates you from the excuse that until there is a perfect solution, you do not need to take action because it would not work for you anyway. The excuse that you are so wonderfully different from everyone else will make you blind to the fact that sometimes things have not worked out for you because you have not taken the appropriate action or that you have avoided admitting that taking consistent action is the only way to improve.

The author of a how-to book or the speaker at a self-improvement seminar does not have to know your precise individual circumstances to be able to help you. It is enough to know that there is a human being trying to achieve something, facing the decisions and challenges thousands of people have faced in similar situations. The critical aspects to focus on, the methods of arriving at the desired outcome, and the supporting beliefs and habits are all universal. These can be applied to your life as they have been applied to the lives of thousands of other people. Never think that you are so unique that you cannot use what other people have learned before you.

## The Feel-Good Factor

*"What a great workshop that was! Oh, I feel so good about myself that I will surely buy one of the speaker's books to get more encouragement and learn more about my amazing potential. And next week, when I have more time on my hands, my new life will begin..."*

We all want to feel good about ourselves. It is not only a nice way to feel, it is also necessary if we are to take consistent action. We are most motivated when we get that good feeling from whatever we are doing and when we feel that we have accomplished something. Then it is easy to keep going and feel that our actions make sense.

For this reason, positive thinking has so often become associated with self-improvement programs. The books, tapes and seminars either directly promote positive thinking or at least want to open up your thinking to all the possibilities in life. Fostering the idea that we are all capable and can achieve our goals in life makes the audience or the reader more receptive to the topics the speaker or the author is presenting. In addition, the best presenters make you laugh, ask you to do funny exercises, tell you touching stories about human potential, make you reflect upon your dreams, and then offer a practical method to break through the barriers that are holding you back. To sum up, they make you feel good about yourself.

However, there is a downside to feeling good. Feeling good is all you may get out of it if you are also not prepared to take consistent action. Feeling good will not make you wealthy, will not make you lose weight, will not find you a soul mate: only taking the right kind of action will.

We all need each other's approval and to know that we are OK. We need someone to tell us that we are in control of what is happening to us, and it is even better when they also assure us that our past shortcomings were really not our fault and can easily be fixed as long as we know the best way to go about it. But feeling good is not enough to make us change our lives. In fact, it may actually limit us by making us too content or placid, leading us to believe that everything is just fine. This feeling of contentedness could be an excuse to think, "Now that I know what wonderful things I am capable of, I will just wait for the right moment and then..."

### The Know-It-Already Fallacy

*"I already know all this. I've heard it many times before.*
*There is no point in listening to it again..."*

Don't read a book or go to a seminar and fall into the "I already know this" trap. If you think about learning as storing information, you are behind the times. The modern theory of learning defines learning as a change in the awareness and action of the learner. When you really learn and process what you know, you will put it into action.

It does not matter what you *know*. What matters is what you *do* with it and what you *become* with this knowledge. If you see the benefit of doing something, yet you are stuck with just knowing it on a cognitive level without actually having done anything, it might be a good idea to hear the message again.

## The Guru Fix

*"She really makes the message come alive in her seminars and gives me energy just by being there. It is so different from only reading about her message in a book by yourself…"*

Many of the so-called motivational gurus are especially very convincing and moving performers. They make things sound very simple, and they are decidedly convinced that their method will work. They make you feel good and capable. They make you believe that you can control your life and that you have great potential. This is what we all want to hear.

Gurus seem to have answers, and when they present their case convincingly, some of their conviction rubs off on you. But trouble will start if you always find yourself needing that conviction from an outside source. The guru fix gets a hold on you when you begin to need regular affirmation from your chosen guru, whom you think embodies the qualities you want to have. You want to hear the gospel and see the method discussed and explained over and over again. There's nothing wrong with this – until you begin to think that only your guru has the answer, and then you begin to think that you always need to hear it directly from that person to really believe it. The problem starts when you become an addict who needs a monthly or yearly "guru fix." This may not be very dangerous, but it is an addiction nevertheless.

Live performances are the main source of getting your "guru fix." You may know what the guru has to say, but the interactivity and emotions make it a performance that you want to watch just for performance's sake. Most importantly, you can share the feeling of being in control of your life and knowing all the answers for a short time with the person who is on stage performing. The guru is the living embodiment of what you want to believe in. When you participate in the group exercises which often push you outside of your normal comfort zone, an emotionally intensive experience is created which gives you the feeling that you have overcome certain hurdles. You get encouragement to take action and your feelings are accepted and validated. It also helps that you are in an environment where any distractions have been eliminated and where you do not have to care about or tend to any other obligations, freeing you up to fully concentrate on the message. When you see it, hear it and feel it with other people, the message becomes very real – much more real than simply reading it in a book.

There is nothing wrong with all this. Live events provide you with a great source of energy to make a change. But bear in mind that *you* are the real source of change in your life, nobody else. You may have the feeling that you've learned and internalized what the guru has to say, but in reality all you may have learned (although you are not aware of it) is that this guru makes you feel good and in addition makes a lot of sense. So the next time you want to make sense of your problems or the world around you, and not to mention feel good, you turn to this guru again. You may not actually be turning to the guru to find the solutions to your problems, but in reality you just might be needing your guru fix. If you have money to spend, that's fine, there's nothing wrong with feeling good, but if you are looking for a genuine solution, beware of this pitfall.

The paradox is that the more we learn from gurus, the less we really need them. If we can take the message, process it and make it our own and then turn it into action, we no longer need to hear the message directly from the guru. And, as we gather knowledge from other sources, we may no longer need to believe in the gurus so unconditionally. Now we can improve on our own. Get comfortable with this idea, and you can get an extra kick from the guru. Just don't transfer your own judgment and ability to take action to someone else.

## The Next Solution Excuse

*"This is the weight loss program that everyone is raving about, so I had better try it...Uh, it did not really work, but maybe that was because I had to give up so many of my favorite foods... Oh well, maybe the book I saw about carbohydrate combining will work better for me..."*

The great thing about our society is that there is always the next solution waiting for you around the corner if you just can't seem to get the results with your present solution. In fact, there are thousands of weight loss methods, success formulas, how-to books, motivational seminars and inspirational audiotapes offering you the next solution.

However, the bad thing about our society is that there is always the next thing waiting for you to pick it up and try it. The thing is, weight loss formulas do not work for you, *you* have to work for you, but because sometimes work is not fun, or we are still holding on to dreams of getting something for nothing, we give up after a few days' trial and then find another method. Maybe it will work next time, but then again, maybe it won't.

Aren't there real differences between all these products on the market, you ask? Sure, there is a world of a difference. However, if you are used to looking for the next solution as an excuse for not really sticking to any of them, none of these choices will really make a difference. Purchasing one self-help book after another just to watch it gather dust on the bookshelf after you've skimmed it through once will lead you nowhere.

## The New Thing Trap

*"This is the latest on sales success. It's only a few months old...how lucky I am that I found it! Now I can find all the up-to-date information that I need to be successful..."*

You are naturally curious about the new. You have also learned that new products are usually more advanced, and therefore, better. While this is true in many cases, it is not always so. What is new is not necessarily better than the old. In fact, it may just be repackaged and have exactly the same contents as before.

Particularly in the area of self-improvement where human nature and people are the main focus, there is rarely a total revolution in the way we think about everything. Improvements are usually small and incremental. What you could learn about human potential ten or twenty years ago is still 100% valid today.

What really needs to be avoided is using new ideas as an excuse not to study what you already have. Newly presented ideas are not always more advanced nor will they always produce better results. What produces results is putting what you already know to work! Don't chase after every new item on the market at the expense of ignoring what is already there.

## The Shelf Help Problem

*"My collection of how-to and self-help books indicates that I really value knowledge. Just using the books as reference guides once in a while will help me to figure out the best way to handle any situation..."*

The trouble with all that advice is that knowing what we should do often will not help us to actually do what we know. Books sitting on your bookshelf, opened once and then forgotten, and thus never acted upon, are not doing you any good. Shelf help won't help.

The reason "shelf help" can quickly get out of hand is this: People, especially intelligent people, often resort to the quick and easy fix which consists of simply searching for additional information on a given subject. When you read an article, check a website or buy a book, you then quickly know something about that subject. The trouble is, you usually stop at this point. You buy another book or set of tapes as a substitute for taking real action. You fool yourself into thinking that by getting more knowledge you have now taken the first step, but if you are honest with yourself, you know that this is as far as you are ever likely to go.

Big companies have the same problem. Most of the knowledge management programs in corporations concentrate on collecting and storing information. Some get as far as distributing it, but very few focus on how to implement the knowledge. Knowing is quite useless if it does not result in better action. Information, whether stored in your head or in your book collection, is not going to do much for you if it just sits there collecting dust on your shelf. Unless you turn it into action or further refine it into wisdom you can share, it is not going to make a much of a difference to your life. Using the information is the key, not collecting it.

In the worst case, having read too many books can even lead to anxiety and a decision to stop reading self-help or how-to books as you feel that you know all there is to know already, yet it still hasn't changed your life in any way.

## The Information Illusion

*"I have read the book so now I know how to proceed. It sounds easy and since I am now so eager to start I'll get straight to it..."*

A little knowledge can be a dangerous thing. If you have only a little knowledge and are eager to apply it all the time, you can get in trouble. Consider the following example: The people who become seriously ill from picking and eating mushrooms that turn out to be poisonous are usually not the beginners (they are extra careful) and not the experts (they know it all). The people who get in trouble are a little further along than the beginners, confident in their abilities, growing bolder by the day, until one day they pick and eat the wrong type of mushroom.

What should you do then? If on one hand you have paralysis by analysis (endlessly preparing for the task) and on the other hand you can get into trouble because of lack of knowledge, what are the options? This is exactly what common sense was invented for. Usually there is no harm done in trying something new. But if there is risk involved, admit it to yourself. When what you are about to embark on concerns your health, involves strenuous physical exercise, is a so-called extreme sport, contains considerable financial risk, or could harm other people, be smart and seek a second opinion.

## The Outside Solution Syndrome

*"I think I know what to do but let me check if there is still something that the experts could tell me..."*

You probably already have the knowledge you need in order to make your life better. But before you move forward, you often want some outside validation. You feel that you need to check if there is something out there that you may not have considered. And of course, there always is. You will always discover something that you did not know. But have you ever stopped to think whether it really makes any difference? Or whether it actually is just taking time away from the activity that you really want to get around to doing in the first place?

Whatever you want to do, the solutions are out there. But in the end, the only thing that makes them work is the process inside you. It makes sense to find out the smart way of doing something or to add to your knowledge. However, this becomes a chore when you feel you have to do it every time before making a decision. By doing so, you are actually making your confidence in your own abilities weaker. Don't become dependent on an external solution. Be bold and do what you already know is right. It will take you further than if you always want to seek an expert's opinion.

## Hey, What About This Book?

Have you at some point of reading through this chapter said to yourself: "Hey, wait a minute, doesn't this also apply to this book?" Isn't this book also potentially just another new thing that you can try out and then move on from? Isn't this book potentially just another "feel-good" product claiming that your failures were not your fault at all, but rather just something that happened because you were not aware of the right techniques to use?

If you've asked yourself some of these questions, congratulations! You are thinking on your own, applying what you read. It is true that this book is not free from the limitations normal self-help and how-to books face. By now you know that it comes with the territory. Keep that same open and active mind-set, think about what makes sense, and you will have no trouble getting past the common pitfalls.

# Dealing with Paradoxes
# and Contradictory Advice

The advice we get from different sources often seems contradictory. The field of self-help is large and you are bound to meet experts who give totally opposing opinions and advice. This is common, and very confusing.

Sometimes the advice itself contains a paradox – a statement that seems to state two opposing ideas that logically cannot both be true at the same time, yet both of these things are in fact true. Why are there so many convincing but contradictory arguments and how should you deal with them?

The first thing to realize is that while there are many ways to do something, no single method is necessarily the best. As you remember from Chapter 4, often just about any kind of action will produce results. There is also a lot of advice that is essentially the same, it is just expressed differently.

Second, the initial confusion may, ironically, lead to the deepest understanding you've had of the idea in question. Consider this paradox as an example: *In order to build, you need to destroy.* It seems to express two totally opposing ideas, but when you think about it, you realize that it simply means that you need to remove the old to make room for the new. It is making a point that when you want to build, you should also think about what already exists and how that affects the process of creating something new.

Paradoxes are not necessarily something to be solved, rather they will increase your understanding when you learn to live with them. Because they present two sides of the coin, they bring balance and give perspective. Contradictory advice is not much different from a paradox. Multiple truths exist and there are many ways to get to your destination.

> *"The test of a first-rate intelligence is the ability to hold two opposed ideas in the mind at the same time, and still retain the ability to function."*
> – F. Scott Fitzgerald

Of course, there will be cases where some advice turns out to be plain wrong and calling it a paradox is not going to change that fact. When you cannot connect two opposing thoughts, you will need to pick the one that feels right to you. If you cannot do that, it is time to discard them both and look for some new ideas.

Consider the following self-improvement paradoxes which show how looking at both sides of an issue creates a new and deeper understanding of the whole.

## Think Big or Take Small Steps?

*"Only big goals produce huge amounts of motivation, so target something that seems almost impossible." vs. "Find a smaller goal that you can easily believe in and achieve."*

On the one hand, this seems to say that unless you get yourself a big hairy goal, you'll have no chance of being motivated enough to ever reach it. The advice states that unrealistic expectations are exactly what you need to get yourself going. However, another piece of advice on goal setting claims that you only have the chance of reaching a goal which you can believe in. In this case the advice states that unrealistic expectations are likely to make you fail and subsequently abandon your improvement efforts. How should you make sense of all this?

Both pieces of advice on goal setting are true, of course. Your realism has led you to where you are at the moment. It is time to become a little bit unrealistic, to imagine what you have not dared to imagine before because you've always viewed it as unrealistic. Yet even a goal that sounds a little unrealistic needs to be broken down into smaller action steps which you can easily believe in.

The size of your goals is a double-edged sword. Let's say that you'd like a new car. You certainly know how to go about getting one: work hard, save money, maybe take out a loan and then you've got your new car! You have the means to realize this goal and you are likely to do so. But what if you want a mansion with a swimming pool and a big impressive garden? Now the majority of us would encounter a problem here. You know that your job does not pay enough to afford such a house and that you must do something dramatically different to make that kind of money. Suddenly, there is no longer any easy means of realizing your goal. There are two kinds of responses: either you give up and settle for a smaller house (because this is more realistic and within your means), or you take up the challenge, get out of your comfort zone and figure out some totally new strategies to increase your earning potential. This is what the self-improvement trainers are trying to get across when they advocate setting huge, almost impossible goals for yourself.

*"You have to think big to make it big." vs.*
*"Everything must be done one step at a time."*

Should you go for the big change cold turkey, start a brand new life, and scrap everything old? Or should you take your time and go forward one step at a time?

Sometimes a radical change is the easiest one. Changing everything at once makes a clean cut and leaves nothing old to cling to. Along with a big change usually comes a new environment in which you are immersed and that new environment carries you forward. Incremental change provides you with excuses. You can always put everything off until tomorrow. A total change leaves you no option but to get it done.

Yet you cannot always start over from scratch and discard everything old. Consider, as an example, that you are living an unhealthy lifestyle. You cannot cast aside your old habits in one day and expect to become healthy. It takes time before you begin to feel the effects of your new diet and exercise routine. And while you're making a focused effort to create a healthier lifestyle, you want stability in other parts of your life – otherwise you'll suffer from overload. So even when you think big, such as "I want to become super-healthy," you will still need to take one step at a time to develop new habits and attitudes.

## Think Positive or Be Realistic?

*"If you feel certain that good things will follow as a result of your actions, they will." vs. "If you are too certain about the actions you are taking, you will miss out on big opportunities to improve."*

Certainty can be described in many ways: confidence, conviction and positive expectations. Being positive increases your chances of taking action. But being too optimistic can also stop you from taking action if you cover up your actual situation with positive thinking and feel no burning desire to change anything. Always being optimistic can mean that you've become content with the situation as it is. When you interpret most things in life positively, you feel no great need to improve. At the same time, if you do not think positively about the possibility of change, you are unlikely to go ahead with it.

Having the conviction that you are doing the right thing propels you to act. Having too much conviction can make you blind to the fact that you might not be taking the right kind of action. Understanding this balance is the key. It is more effective to be sure that you will ultimately reach your goals than to be convinced that your current actions are the best or the only way of achieving them.

## Focus Your Efforts or Create Options?

*"If you want to get really good at something, you need to concentrate all your efforts on reaching that one goal." vs. "Balanced development is the key to living a successful life."*

You see athletes and other top performers single-mindedly pursuing success in their chosen field. You see that they are very skilled and successful at what they are doing, yet in self-help books you are often given the advice to strive for balanced development instead of superior performance in just one area. Many books tell you that the concentration of power and focus is what brings the rewards, yet at the same time they advise you to balance your development. How can you do both?

Even those athletes who focus on just one sport still do all types of different exercises to improve their overall ability as an athlete. Modern sports science encourages coaches to expose the athlete to a wide variety of different sports and exercises to build up their overall athletic capability. Pete Sampras, who won more Grand Slam tennis tournaments in the 1990s than any other player, was enrolled in a ballet class when he was young to develop his overall coordination. Similarly, you can see ice hockey players enrolled in aerobics classes to maintain their mobility.

Balanced development will enrich your life by giving you more choices. Yet once you decide which direction you are going to take, you'll need to focus on following that particular path, otherwise you will never get anywhere.

*"Only concentrate on what you can really succeed in. If you can't do something well, then it's not worth doing at all." vs.*
*"Do everything as well as you can. Everything counts."*

There are always more things to do than your time and resources permit. It makes sense to focus your efforts on the key things that will make the biggest difference in your life. Spreading your energies too thin will not lead to good results in anything. Yet your life is filled with little things that should also be done.

The key is to realize that sometimes it is the little things that matter the most. Often it is the tiny differences that determine how high you can reach. The world of sports and business is full of stories about how the most mundane detail, when ignored, turned out to be the reason for failure. When everybody is focused on getting the big things right, the differences at that level can be non-existent. The decisive factor is sometimes who has enough energy and motivation to take care of the little things as well.

*"Work on your strengths – only they will give you an advantage."*
*vs. "Work on your weaknesses. The chain is only as strong as its weakest link."*

Which advice should you believe: Work on making your strengths even stronger or work on improving your weaknesses?

In a world where careers tend to be more specialized than ever, sharpening your stronger qualities to the point where you are able to perform them superbly is likely to bring you a competitive advantage. This view proclaims that you have to select an area where you want to reach a level of excellency and do just enough in other areas to make sure that these areas do not stand in the way of progress. Of course, this can lead to one-sided development, leaving you with no options if something unexpected happens (think of a dedicated athlete who loses his or her health in an accident and then struggles to find a new career with little education and no work experience).

Balanced development will offer more options and make you flexible in various situations. However, if you are not particularly strong in any one area, potential employers, for example, may find it difficult to "categorize" you and offer you a job that matches your abilities. But life is not just about careers and comparing your abilities with those of other people. What matters most is what brings you the greatest joy – whether it is a very narrow and specialized field or whether it consists of the broader development of all your abilities.

## To Trust Your Instincts or Not to Trust Them?

*"Your body will know what is right for you." vs. "You cannot always trust your instincts."*

Often it seems that there is no contest here. Most people and a large number of self-help programs would advise you to trust your instincts and do what feels right for you. This is true in many cases – your mind and body are incredibly aware and tuned in and you should not discount the signals they give you – but there are important exceptions to this rule.

First, we really haven't developed our instincts in certain areas, although we may think otherwise. Nobody is born with any instincts whatsoever about money, for example. We learn about money as we grow up, but there is no guarantee that what we have learned is correct. Countless dollars have been lost because somebody did not bother to check the facts and instead trusted their instincts to tell them which investment to make.

Second, sometimes your body craves certain things, making it seem that this is really what you need, when in fact, it may badly need just the opposite. Don't trust your body when it craves nicotine or chocolate because you had a bad day at work. It is possible that you have created a dependency which is ultimately harmful to you. For example, some studies suggest that many people in western countries suffer from a form of sugar addiction that is aggravated by frequent snacks, soft drinks and processed food, leading to an imbalance of insulin secretion which in turn leads to many health problems. The sugar fix your body craves in this state is exactly what it should not have.

The point is, the next time you crave something, don't automatically think that your body knows best. Sure, if you are thirsty you should have something to drink and not second-guess your feelings, but many things are more complex than that. Your body and mind are adaptive systems and sometimes they adapt to less than optimal situations. Trusting your instincts is good self-help advice but not when you fail to look at the big picture and consider other alternatives as well.

## Counterintuitive Advice

Some of the best advice is counterintuitive. We all have our normal ways of thinking and when someone challenges them by providing a totally new angle of looking at things, we are given a chance to learn tremendously. Here are five examples of counterintuitive advice that apply to personal development.

*"You learn the most from the material you already know."*

Unlike fiction, non-fiction books get better the more often you read them. The best thing is to read many books covering the same topic, delving deeper and deeper into it. Thus you learn the most not from totally new material, but from the material that is already familiar. Real learning is not about information, it is about using knowledge to make changes in your behavior. The material you remember, process and apply the fastest is material that you already have the mental structures for. Reread the same how-to books over and over again to get the most out of them. When you begin to recognize the underlying patterns of thought and find dozens of applications to your own life, you know that you have understood the heart of the matter.

*"You will have more energy if you don't stop to rest."*

Action energizes your mind and body. If you are tired after a day of work, the surefire way to lose all your energy is to slump on the couch and "rest." Breaks are necessary, and you need rest if you are exhausted, but taking a break just for the sake of it will bring all the momentum to a halt, making it hard to get going again. Both your body and your brain were designed for activity; mental and physical energies are interconnected. So, do not stop – you will ultimately find it easier to maintain higher energy levels and your momentum if you keep going.

*"If you really want to succeed you need to fail continuously."*

The paradox of self-improvement is that it shows you at your best and it shows you at your worst. Why? Because striving to improve means that you are taking action, taking risks, doing things you have not done before and invariably, at some point you are going to fail, look bad or just feel really stupid. It's OK – this is the price you have to pay to reap the rewards and often there is no way around it. So smile to yourself and say, "Well, don't I feel stupid!" and then move on. As long as you learn from this experience, the more you fail, and the earlier you fail, the more chances of success you will have in the future.

*"The faster you push yourself to work, the better*
*the quality will be."*

This flies in the face of all the common sense which dictates that you need time for quality. This is true, of course, and some things can only work with time. There is, however, another aspect to consider. When you know that your time is limited, you are forced to pick out the things that really matter and concentrate your efforts on them. You simply have no time for the not-so-important stuff; you get straight to the heart of the matter. Your sense of what is valuable use of your time becomes heightned when you must actively decide what you are going to spend it on. This in turn creates quality because often there are only a few key elements that really make a difference and all the rest is just superfluous. Rest assured that if you had all the time in the world to read how-to books, your results in life would not be that much better than if you only could spend one tenth of that time but were still really motivated to make the best out of it.

*"If you try hard to do the best you can, you will never achieve that great success that you are dreaming of."*

It is not really fair, but simply doing what you can do is rarely enough. It has brought you to your present situation. You can get to the very top only if you try hard to do what you cannot do and don't want to do. You don't have to grit your teeth and do something horribly unpleasant. But you do have to do something you have never done before and be willing to face the uncertainty that comes with it. The best way to expand your comfort zone is to leave it behind!

# 13.

# Breaking Through the Barriers to Success

What are the things that stop you short of success? Why, despite all the good intentions and plenty of advice, do you still run up against a wall in your attempts to improve your life? There are a number of self-improvement barriers that prevent you from achieving what you want. This chapter brings together the most common reasons for not succeeding in your efforts to change. The purpose of this collection is to help you identify and deal with the bottlenecks that may be slowing you down or stopping your progress altogether.

Some issues will disappear as soon as you recognize that they merely exist. You may even laugh at how such a "little thing" has been holding you back. Other things may require more effort to work through, but there are always books, tapes and trainers who offer their help in dealing with those issues.

There is one danger with this list. If you were shown a long list of the symptoms of the most common illnesses, you would almost certainly find something that matches your current condition, although there is really nothing wrong with you. In a similar fashion, you could find so many reasons to fail from this chapter that you would begin to believe that you will never succeed. In reality, there are only a few barriers which are stopping your progress, and once you've identified what they are, you can find ways to get rid of them. Very often, what is stopping you is just confusion resulting from something unexpected. This chapter will clear up that confusion so you can find a solution and avoid the same problem in the future.

### The Social Barrier: People Around You

When you change, the people around you will react to you differently. You are no longer quite the same person, and they'll wonder whether they know you anymore. They may behave differently, they may question your judgment, they may complain that you only pay attention to yourself, they may tell your other friends that you have become a little weird and they may begin to withdraw their love and affection from you. They are doing this because the changes you have made in your life make them feel uncomfortable, even insecure – your change pushes them outside of their comfort zone, and that is something they are not prepared for. You have the benefit of knowing what you are doing, but they have no idea what is happening, so it is no wonder they may react negatively.

When this happens (and it happens often!), you may retreat back to your old behavior, not wanting to upset the social aspect of your life. You may even be so conscious of the likelihood of this kind of situation that you never even begin any attempt to change at all. But the fact is, if you change, people around you need to change as well. People you feel connected to are people who are similar to you. If you change a great deal, this balance no longer exists. Some relationships may never be the same again, but most people will understand when you explain this and spend time with them. If you lose too many connections, it was probably time to find some new friends anyway.

Consider the effect of your change on other people before you begin. Nothing happens in a vacuum and the smartest way to change is to involve other people, not to exclude them. Make sure that there are people in your life who give encouragement and support. Acknowledge that you could expect some discouragement from others, but do not let that stop you.

### The Rules Barrier: Creating a Game You Can't Win

We all have rules for ourselves. They give us the criteria to evaluate our actions. If you feel that you've never succeeded in anything, you have probably created too many rules for yourself to follow. You feel that everything has to be done according to the rules you've made before you can call anything a success. You may think that in order to be happy, you have to fulfill all the criteria ("I cannot be happy unless I have a family, a career, a beautiful house, and all at once"). Of course, with all these rules going unfulfilled, you never feel that you've succeeded in anything, and you begin to resent having to take any action because you know what the outcome is already.

One reason you may have too many rules for yourself is because you are trying to create an ideal life. Don't take the self-help exercises for "the ideal self" too literally. Your ideal life can be a model to motivate you, but you will always be a work in progress. Trying to be perfect puts a tremendous pressure on yourself because as a rule you can almost never successfully carry it out.

Ease up. Life is not a game that has to be played according to a set of rules, like checkers or another boardgame; it is more like children's free-flowing, spontaneous play where the game and rules are sort of invented as you go along. Lots of strict and inflexible rules just get in the way of playing. When you take up self-improvement efforts, be aware of the rules you set for success and failure. A typical problem is to characterize success as a decidedly big achievement, and then being ready to pronounce every little hiccup as failure. Don't measure yourself in a way that makes it virtually impossible to succeed. And first of all, get rid of the rule that claims that you cannot be happy with yourself if you don't follow all the rules!

## The Dialogue Barrier: Talking to Yourself

We all have an internal dialogue, that conversation we have when we talk to ourselves. This dialogue can create a barrier to success when it is inconsistent or uses only part of the means or resources available.

What we forget is that while our internal dialogue is going on, similar to one-to-one communication, the words themselves are only one minor part of the message. What we feel, how we stand, breathe, walk, look or flex our muscles communicates as much to ourselves as to the outer world. One reason we fail to change is that we intellectually understand the need for change but we do not put our feelings and non-verbal communication behind this need as well. When we then begin to take action, we somehow feel that we are not fully behind the effort. This is because our internal dialogue keeps sending mixed messages. We need to be behind our our effort to change 100%, involving all aspects of ourselves.

We can use our inner dialogue to tell us what we should do, and to cheer ourselves on. But similar to what often happens in the outside world, we also internally resist being told what to do. We can only succeed if we are emotionally, intellectually and physically consistent. You cannot believe yourself to be full of energy if you are slumping on the couch, no matter how much you may believe this idea intellectually.

How to snap out of this then? If you "don't feel like it," the most effective way to change the way you feel is to change your mental and physical state at the same time. The next time you don't feel like going to work when you wake up in the morning, remember that no amount of thinking about it in your bed is going to make much of a difference. But when you get up and do it, involving your body and your mind, it isn't so bad and afterwards you usually end up feeling pretty good about yourself.

### The Discomfort Barrier: Feeling Uncertain and Insecure

Change can produce uncertainty and insecurity. When you have decided to leave your old ways behind and make a change, you may feel a little uncomfortable for two reasons. You know that your old habits were not perfect, but you also know that your new way of behaving has not yet proven itself. Realize that everybody has these feelings. Acknowledging this as a normal part of the change process will already give you a sense of control over the situation.

If you always try to stay safe, you will limit your potential dramatically. You know how your present world works, and even when it is not always fun, you know what to expect and how to handle things. So you may even keep on doing the same old things that you really don't want to do, instead of focusing on what you really do want, because these familiar things give you a sense of security.

You don't have to like the uncertainty that comes with change, but once you understand that trying to stay safe by never getting out of your comfort zone will also eventually lead to frustration, it is then easier to accept some insecurity. Ultimately your actions will then create a new feeling of security because you know that you are capable of much more than before.

### The Procrastination Barrier: Short-Term Satisfaction

The reason you find it hard to change is that it requires a firm decision and a sustained effort. Unfortunately, many of us have taught ourselves that we do not have to take our own decisions seriously. Instead of getting to the task at hand we have learned to procrastinate. We do it because it feels good. For a moment we feel that we are in control of our life, that we can choose. When your logic gets twisted, you may even begin to need the satisfaction you feel from procrastinating; you use it to convince yourself that although you never get things done, the reason is that there is just so much to do in your life. You fool yourself by thinking that you are so busy *living* that you just couldn't possibly begin to do what you really need to get done.

We make a lot of decisions but do not follow through on them. We teach ourselves that although we've decided to do something, it doesn't necessarily mean that we are going to go through with it. By doing this, we create a condition where we begin to disregard the importance of decisions. Telling yourself that you should do something, and then doing nothing, is a surefire way of losing your self-esteem and becoming anxious and frustrated.

Think of yourself as your own customer. How many times are you going to forget all the broken promises you've made to yourself before all your confidence in yourself is gone? Make fewer decisions, and if you really have trouble keeping them, enlist outside help that will help you stay on the right track. If going through with big decisions is troublesome, break them down into smaller tasks. Sometimes it is helpful not to begin with a decision at all, but to experiment with some action and see if that moves you closer to making a decision you can finally keep.

### The Overload Barrier: Taking It Too Seriously

Being so committed to your personal development program that it begins to dominate your whole life is taking it too seriously. Evaluating every single minute spent, task completed or person met on the basis of whether or not it moves you towards your goals is taking it far too seriously. Not only will people think that you have gone nuts, but more importantly, by doing so you are actually getting less out of your efforts rather than more.

Optimizing every minute will not optimize your performance. You need time to rest and let your mind process things. It is during these periods of rest that the mind and body recuperate and become stronger. Putting yourself under constant stress and pressure will not produce growth; it will lead to a mental and physical breakdown.

A way of taking it all too seriously is to let the self-help and how-to advice "invent" you. It is a different matter to internalize the ideas (a good thing) than to begin to live your life in terms of checklists and techniques and to consider those as your ideal self (not such a good thing). Separate the schedules, plans and written goals from who you are as a person. They are the structure you need to adhere to, but do not let them become the essence of who you are. They are not your identity.

### The Expectations Barrier:
### Trying to Get It Right the First Time

If your expectation is to succeed perfectly the first time, you are naturally going to see any effort you make as a failure. Rarely, if ever, do you get it right the first time you try. This is just not the way things work. If you are ready to pronounce something a failure after one try, maybe you should admit to yourself that you are really just looking for an excuse not to try anything new. Modify your expectations. Expect that any improvement will take some time, but that you *can* and *will* eventually master it.

Compare what you are trying to do with learning to ride a bicycle. Children are determined that they are also going to learn to ride when they see other kids riding their bicycles. So they try, and they fail, and they try again, and of course they succeed. They succeed because it would not occur to them in a million years to blame the bike for not working. It may be awkward, difficult and frustrating, but somehow they know that it is up to them to learn to ride. And then they do it, just like that!

Often, the more important your goal is to you, the less your skills and getting it "right" really matter. Many things are not about the perfect or ideal outcome, they are more about beginning a journey that will take us towards what we want to be and what we would like to have in life. Your relationship with someone you love is not about the skills that would make it perfect, it is about caring enough that you will always make the effort, whether you happen to get it right or not.

## The Motivation Barrier: Not Knowing What You Want

If you don't feel motivated, it is hard to take consistent action that will bring about long-term results. To create lasting motivation, you need to know what you want, why you want it, and what is required in order to get there.

The most common reason for a lack of motivation is *trying to want* something that you really *don't* want. Somehow you decided on a goal that is not really what you want at all. Perhaps it was peer pressure, maybe it was what your parents wanted for you or maybe it was the self-help guru who said that your ultimate goals should be peace, love and happiness (certainly good goals in themselves). Whatever it was, this particular goal is not what you really wanted and as a result, all the books, seminars and coaches will serve only as an external, not internal, source of motivation.

Pause to examine your own dreams – you owe it to yourself. You need to know why you want something. When you have come up with enough reasons, you will then become very empowered. At some level, however vague, you also need to know what is required to get what you want. If you don't know where to begin, your efforts will soon falter.

To get motivated you have to begin somewhere and take action to make your motivation grow. Motivation creates more motivation. It grows best in interaction with people and the surrounding world, not in isolation.

Motivation becomes stronger with the fewer conflicting beliefs you have. A classical example is that you are looking for a career change, finally doing what you really love, but not recognizing that at the same time your beliefs motivate you to avoid insecurity, uncertainty and financial risk. Your contradictory beliefs weaken your motivation and resolve to take decisive action because you know that making a career change will force you to deal with many things you have never faced before. When you are unaware of this, you feel very uneasy because whatever you decide, part of your beliefs system is going to work against it and make you feel uncomfortable.

### The Willpower Barrier: Trying to Force Things

If you always require a lot of willpower to take action and to focus on the task at hand, you are doing something wrong. Your motivation, not your willpower, should focus you. When your thoughts and actions are aligned with your beliefs and your identity, you'll find a natural way to focus. If you have to constantly force yourself to do things, you are probably not very clear on what you want in life, why you want it, and what it takes to get it.

When you know what you are doing and doing what you love in life, you'll find an easy rhythm to your actions. You still have to do things that you don't like to do, and at those times you can get the necessary boost from willpower. But you cannot operate on willpower alone – it consumes huge amounts of mental energy and breaks the natural rhythm. Use the power of beliefs, habits, self-identity and externalizations to support getting things done. When you enjoy what you do, it is easy to focus on what you are doing. People who are really good at what they do rarely use willpower as their main source of energy for achieving things. They let it flow from who they are.

The time to use willpower is when you face a moment of truth. This may be the brief moment when you must decide which course of action you are going to take. Use willpower in following situations:

- To set things in motion. To break through the inertia that is maintaining the status quo.
- To wait for your "second wind." Sometimes you are exhausted but know that if you just hang in there for a few more moments, things will start getting better again.
- To complete the "last repetition." As in lifting weights, pushing yourself just a little bit further for that one last repetition provides you with all the growth.

Rather than "staying focused" all day long, you need to focus for brief moments hundreds of times – and here willpower can help. During those moments you need to actively make decisions that will take you closer to your goals. Willpower will help you to stay on the right track when you are tired, distracted or tempted by something else, and it can help you complete those unpleasant tasks that simply need to be done. But willpower should only be one of the tools in your toolbox, not the one you rely on for all the jobs you have to do!

### The Time Barrier: Waiting for the Perfect Moment

If you feel that you have to wait for the perfect moment to begin, you are just using this as an excuse to postpone the activity. It can also be a sign that you don't really know what you want to do. If you value what you are doing, if it's really important to you, then you do not have to wait for the perfect moment. When you are doing what you love, it does not matter if there are distractions because you hardly notice them. We all have had experiences when we were so enthralled by an activity that time flew by and we were in complete and utter concentration, noticing nothing else.

As long as you know what you want, there is no reason to wait. Now is the perfect moment to begin. Getting going will give you more energy. Don't let the intention die. Do anything, but just do it.

### The Energy Barrier: Exhausting Yourself

Without energy it is impossible to maintain a sustained effort. Because mental and physical energies are connected, you need to take care of both to have enough power to reach your goals. The simple reason you stop working is that you are tired. Even when you really want to do something and you understand the importance of it, if you begin to feel exhausted, you pull back. And as you stop, you may lose all the momentum you were working so hard to build up. Willpower may help a few times, your motivation may get you to carry on for a while, but they cannot replace the physical energy that is lacking.

A limited amount of energy will also cause you to avoid those actions which have the possibility of failure included in them. Limited energy makes you overly cautious. When you come home after a hard day's work and feel completely beat, the last thing you have motivation for is trying something new. After all, those things could fail and then the last ounce of energy you have would be wasted. Better turn on the TV and relax a little...

If you feel tired more often than you should, buy a book on how to get more energy and put it to action. You owe it to your dreams to energize yourself.

### The Complacency Barrier: Good Enough Is Not Good Enough

If you are a person who has already achieved some success in life, it may be harder for you to change than for anybody else.

If you belong to this group, you have a career, a good education, a circle of like-minded friends and perhaps a family. You have collected a fair number of possessions, you have some money in the bank and enjoy the status as a good worker with a steady job. You have already earned a fair amount in life, and you know that if you keep working in the same way, you will steadily increase the material goods in your life. Yet you somehow have this nagging feeling that you are not getting as much out of your efforts as you should be, and you may even feel a little trapped in your job and normal circumstances. You would like to make a change in your life, but whatever you try, somehow you're never quite able to stick to it.

Interestingly, this describes a large number of the readers of how-to and self-help books. People who already have many sales skills buy the most sales books and attend the most workshops. People who already are in touch with their feelings and have thought about their values are the biggest buyers of books on those topics. They are already doing fairly well, but they know that they could be doing a lot better. They feel that although they have already met their basic material needs, they crave a better balance between their private life, their work, and their aspirations. People who already have achieved a fair degree of success are often frustrated because they can only envision the traditional way of getting more – by working harder and longer – and they want smarter ways to deal with their life.

If you belong to this group, the biggest obstacle you may have preventing you from making a change is that you have already settled for the "good enough" status quo in your life. Your present "success" is what keeps you from getting better. When you come home after working a ten-hour day and still bring home paperwork for the weekend – perhaps the very thing you wanted to change – it is easy to give in to the temptation of wanting some freedom and relaxation. You switch on the TV instead of working a little more on your future. And when you fail to make an effort, your comfortable life provides you with an easy excuse for not taking any self-improvement failures seriously – "It wasn't that important anyway and my life is actually pretty good." In fact, you may even secretly pride yourself on the fact that none of this "self-help stuff" has had any effect on you.

You are so content with your present life that although you would like to improve it, you want to do it with minimum hassle (just a little precision guided improvement here, please). But things are interconnected and making a real change will bring some hassle with it. You will have to change your schedule, say "no" to that social function, admit that not everything in your present life is going OK, maybe get some odd looks from your friends, and live with the uncertainty that the change brings. And all the while your comfortable "old life" keeps calling you back!

If you give in to the temptation and settle for good enough, you will never get the chance to find anything else which could be better. To gather the necessary momentum for a change in this kind of a situation, you need to understand why it is hard for you to change; accept that if you don't, you will always feel a little frustrated. Work on your self-motivation by creating enough reasons for improvement and enlist other people to help you stick to your new habits.

# PART THREE

# FROM ADVICE TO ACTION: MAKING A LASTING CHANGE IN YOUR LIFE

**14.**

# Putting Advice into Practice

The third part of this book deals with putting the available self-help and how-to resources to work. It explains how you can make sure that you achieve what you are looking for in life. Learn the six leverage points described in this chapter, then use the elements for lasting change which are described in the following chapters – and you will see real results from the advice you receive, every time.

The first thing to do when creating a lasting change in your life is to stop believing in miraculous self-improvement shortcuts. They do not exist. We know this, yet we do not want to believe it. You get what you pay for. You have to put in the effort to produce the results. One of the reasons you fail is because you refuse to believe what you already know.

This is so obvious, yet most people in their pursuit of a quick-fix solution choose to ignore it. We want the miracle cure, the effortless results because then we don't have to confront our own shortcomings. Rather than facing up to our own actions, we go looking for the next promise.

But it's not always your personal shortcomings that cause you to fail. Sometimes there are shortcomings in the advice which makes it difficult for you to put the advice to use. And if one program "fails," you may erroneously think that what you need to do now is buy additional books or tapes. But if these materials as well do not contain information on how to learn what they teach, you are unlikely to move towards your goals any faster.

Instead of shortcuts, what has been often missing is the most effective way of using the self-help and how-to resources that are already available. This book you're now holding in your hands can act as a guide to realizing that potential, but it is still you who has to initiate action. Nobody else holds that power.

The most important thing is to trust yourself. You already know what you need to do and how to do it. When you also accept that there are no shortcuts, the feeling will be very liberating. You can stop chasing after every new book on dieting. You no longer have to worry about the latest life management technique. And if you do rush out to buy that new book, you know how to get the most out of it.

Ironically, the only shortcut that exists is to stop wasting time on shortcuts and start doing what really works.

### Do What Works: The Four Truths and Six Leverage Points

If you find yourself wondering whether you have what it takes to begin and keep up the effort to make your life better, remember these four self-improvement truths:

First of all, you already know *what brings results*. You know it initially takes courage to begin, support from others, some planning and consistent action. Start with what you have, right now, and do what you can, right now. Often you do not need to go looking for a totally new solution, a new book or new set of cassettes. What you need to do is to just begin.

Secondly, you already have a great deal of *resources*. Don't fool yourself into thinking that you cannot get what you want because you lack resources. You already have many resources: You have some money, you have time, and you have friends and colleagues. You have an education, motivation, abilities, knowledge, courage, faith, dreams, self-discipline, and you have determination. Make the best use of what you have, and you'll be surprised at what you get back for your efforts!

Thirdly, you already have *energy*. All you need to get started is to use this energy during the few key moments of your day when you are working towards your goals. You do not have to stay energetic and focused all day long – just for a brief moment at the right time. You will find that taking action towards your dreams actually produces more energy than it consumes.

Fourthly, you already have *time*. There is never a better time to begin taking action than right now. Starting a new habit doesn't take long. Most of your day may be filled with routine tasks that simply have to be done, but you only need a moment. You need to decide what is important to you. Don't let yourself be fooled into thinking that you have no time. You can find the time when what you want becomes important enough.

Keep in mind the abovementioned four truths and follow the six leverage points listed below to get better results from any self-help or how-to program:

1. Work from your own agenda.
2. Enlist help from other people.
3. Follow a system.
4. Work a little bit better, but consistently.
5. Be in control, but have some faith, too.
6. If it is not working, stop.

### Leverage Point 1: Work from Your Own Agenda

You get a surge of motivation and energy from working towards your own goals which you have set for yourself for your own personal reasons. Remember, if you are not working according to your own agenda or plan, you are working from somebody else's. It is not a good idea to simply desire or wish for what everybody else wants, find out what you want. When you understand why you are doing something and why it is so important to you, you will never lack self-motivation.

Your agenda includes a list of the main issues and priorities you need to work on. Setting your own agenda is important because you will never have enough time to do everything. Invariably, you need to make trade-offs and decide which activities to spend time on. Beginning a personal development effort might mean taking time off from watching television, missing out on other entertainment opportunities or even not seeing your friends once in a while. Making decisions about your time is easy when you are aware of what you are trying to achieve, but it is terribly frustrating when you feel like you're trying to realize someone else's dreams instead of your own. Pause to reflect upon what it is that you really want and need at this moment.

Information overload and too much work can leave you feeling that outside or external events have control over you. Your own agenda will give you control over your life. When you know your priorities, you regain your sense of control. You will also find that when you are working for yourself, even long workweeks don't lead to burnout.

Avoid doing anything that is not on your agenda. Deliberately put things on your agenda, even when they are handed to you from outside (sometimes you have no choice in the matter – if your house is on fire, it becomes your number one priority to get out safely no matter what other important things are on your agenda). Always set your own agenda and guard it very, very carefully because this is what your life is made up of.

### Leverage Point 2: Enlist Help from Other People

Enlisting help is the best way to speed up the realization of your dreams. But getting help, ironically, is the most under-estimated part of self-help. The very word "self-help" leads us astray. Nobody has enough knowledge, skills and willpower to do it all alone. Nor does it make any sense. When you find people to support you and when you in turn become committed to them, you will do more with them and for them than you would ever manage to do alone.

Always doing things alone and never telling anyone protects you from embarrassment in case you fail, but it also makes fail-ure more likely. When nobody is around to keep an eye on you, it is all too easy to find excuses and too hard to keep going when your own energy and determination falter. It is too easy to get confused and begin to wonder if any of it makes any sense. Do not fall into the trap of not asking for help because it makes you feel weak or challenges your self-image or identity as a person who can handle things him/herself. Asking for help is a sign of strength – only a strong person has the courage to be open enough to approach someone for help.

Don't depend on your own willpower alone. Ask other people to help you, to cheer you on, or even force you to continue when your own motivation falters. Top athletes have someone to encourage them to go one more lap, to do one more repetition, and if necessary, to even drag them out of bed on a really bad day. You need to have such a person in your life, too. If it is important enough to you that you have made it your goal, it is important enough to get other people to help you.

Be smart and don't ask people what they know about something – the last thing you're likely to need is more information! Lack of knowledge is rarely our true problem. In most cases we more or less know what should be done but we just cannot get ourselves to do it or stick to it. Ask people just to help you take action and to support you if your own self-discipline fails. This will certainly get you a few peculiar looks, as most people never ask for this kind of help. Yet people already know how to give this kind of support; they offer it when you become ill, when someone loses their job or when someone is recovering from a loss. They encourage you to carry on and not give up. Strangely, this kind of help is rarely offered to people who have nothing wrong with them, but who are just trying to improve themselves further.

A book, a tape or a seminar can supply you with information and the initial nudge to take the first steps. But most of the time you are alone when you need to be taking consistent action, which is the most critical step of all. Rarely can words on paper drag you out of bed or remind you to take your daily dose of action. Additionally, most of us are not well trained to cheer ourselves up and we do not feel quite at ease praising ourselves for a job well done. For the lack of this kind of support, it is all too easy to feel that our self-improvement effort did not quite bring all that we were expecting. Congratulating ourselves is fine, but the celebration party would sure be a lot more fun if somebody else was involved as well.

We not only fail because we do not seek help, but also because we enlist it in the wrong phase. We may get help in the beginning, taking a friend with us to a seminar, or agreeing to go for a run together, or getting our spouse to take care of the kids while we try out a new activity. But the most difficult part is not really at the beginning. When we attend a seminar and are filled with enthusiasm we can usually get started by ourselves and maintain our efforts for the first couple of weeks or months. However, we often run out of energy and begin to backslide after a few weeks. Your "helpful friend" is already busy with something else and your spouse is demanding that household tasks be taken care of. On top of that, it may be a little embarrassing to admit that the "new life" you were going to start is not proceeding very well.

This is the most difficult moment. You are in the middle of it all, the initial excitement is gone and you have not arranged for help for "the second month." Most people fail to recognize that we need the most help in the middle, and that we should plan ahead for that help before we need it. Once you get past the second or third month, you have usually established the new habit and are unlikely to need so much support anymore. But to get that far, you often need someone to help you during the challenging middle phase as well.

Don't overdo the help or support you receive in the very beginning unless you really have trouble getting up from the couch and doing anything. Plan ahead and get someone to help you in the middle – that is when you'll find that you are closest to giving up. Don't be home alone at the most critical moment. Get all the help you can. Your goals are worth it.

### Leverage Point 3: Follow a System

Have you ever heard about a sport where you can get to the very top training whichever way you want and whenever you feel like it without a well-thought out plan? Or have you ever heard of a company that followed any old course of action and still became a success story? Of course not! You need to be systematic to get to any meaningful results.

The system is the solution. It will focus you, it will act as a reminder list, and it will bring structure to your efforts. Buy, build, borrow or steal a system that will support your growth. There is no need to figure it all out on your own, especially when you are in the beginning phases and there is little benefit from improvising until you have mastered the basics. Start with a ready-made system. Find out what you need to know, what the right way of doing things is, what pitfalls to avoid and how to make it all fun. You can use a system described in a book, video or seminar, join a club, take a course or get a personal coach.

By all means experiment and try out several approaches to find the one that works best for you. But for many things there isn't a great number of alternatives. Although there are different ways of doing things, usually only a handful of tested methods produce the best results in any given area. Those are the systems you should be on the look out for (use the resource list at the end of this book for some suggestions).

"System" also means the environment in which you live.

Situations and structures either support or hinder your personal development efforts. Put yourself in a situation that carries you forward – enroll in a class, get help from your friends, make a family commitment, or join an organization. The support and structure you get will make the bad days seem not quite so bad and the good days feel really good when you can share it with others. Steer clear of situations that do not support you and your efforts. For example, if your social life centers around a hard-partying and chain-smoking circle of friends, you are not likely to receive much support for your new fitness habit. On the other hand, if you join a sports club or gym and get a friend to join with you, you will find that your environment continously sends you signals that supports your getting into shape.

When you are aware of which area you want to improve upon and get some personal experience in this area, you can begin to create a system of your own. Maybe you no longer want to call it a system at all when you have internalized the ideas and find a way to apply them to your daily life. When Arnold Schwarzenegger described his bodybuilding training, he said that he first systematically recorded everything to be able to analyze it, but after years of training, he instinctively knew what to do, what would be effective, and then he no longer needed to be so programmatic.

No system will always work or work forever. And there is no need to try to program your whole life – you need spontaneity to enjoy life and to take advantage of the opportunities that present themselves. But a system will always get you started more effectively than working without one.

### Leverage Point 4: Work a Little Bit Better, But Consistently

Small improvements, compounded over time, will lead to monumental changes in your life. Consistency will work wonders where a single burst of effort fails to produce results. Consistency will guarantee lasting results whereas the quick-fix gives you a fast high but drops you back to the ground with the blink of an eye.

You do not need to be ten times more effective than you are now to get ten times better results. In sports, the winner is often better by a fraction of a second, yet they get the prize instead of those who were almost as good. Similarly, in your life, that small extra effort, over time, will lead to disproportionately high rewards.

You get extraordinary results from consistency for three reasons. First, progress is not always linear. When you are getting started in any new activity you will spend a lot of time learning the ropes. Once you are well on your way, everything becomes more efficient, and you learn more and more with the same amount of effort. Second, you are not doing things in a vacuum. Once you begin to change, the world around you begins to change. You will get help and support from others which will multiply the effect of your own efforts. Third, the compounded effects of your efforts will be stored in your mind and body. If you take a two-week break from the fitness program that you have been following for a year, you can easily go back to it afterwards and will not have lost the effects. But if you take a two-week break at the very beginning of your new fitness program, going back to it afterwards will feel like starting everything all over again.

It is the small things, repeated over time, that make a difference. You just don't run a thousand miles a year to get into shape:

you run five miles three times a week for a year. Break big things into smaller chunks that are easier to handle. Don't set the goal of losing twenty pounds in a month, set a goal of losing one pound per week for the next twenty weeks. The results are guaranteed to be easier to achieve and to last longer.

### Leverage Point 5: Be In Control But Have Some Faith, Too

When you want to improve your life, you need to decide that you are in control of it. Your choices determine what you get out of it. At the same time, you need to have faith that the actions you take are moving you in the right direction, even if the going gets tough and you begin to doubt the purpose of it all. A sense of control is necessary to allow you to steer yourself towards your dreams, but you also need a sense of faith to believe that things will turn out well for you.

You are not always entirely free to choose what you do in the short term, or capable of getting what you want without a great deal of effort, but ultimately, you are the only person in control of what happens in your life. You need to be able to believe that you can "self-regulate" yourself, that things don't just happen to you, that you make them happen by your own thoughts and actions. When you are able to operate as an autonomous person, you will create a strong sense of internal motivation to go after your goals – after all, you set these goals. Decide to take active control of your life. Nobody else will do it for you.

Control does not mean that you can dictate exactly what happens. It is more of a feeling of being able to affect things in a way that makes a difference and to be able to work with what happens. You cannot control all the events around you, but you can decide how you react to them, how you make sense of them, and how you work with them.

You need faith to see a little further and to trust your actions. Consider for a moment that you were not aware of the positive effects of jogging on your health. If you were then given advice to try it a few times, and you did, the only immediate feedback you would get from this activity would be sore and aching muscles. You would conclude that this is detrimental to your health and never consider jogging again. This would happen because you were only experiencing the short-term discomforts but not understanding and having faith in the long-term benefits.

Most importantly, you need to have faith at the moment of failure, when despite your best efforts things did not work out the way you had wanted. You need to have faith that this failure will not stop you from reaching your goals. People are not successful because they do not fail, people are successful because when they fail, they try again. Faith will carry you over the rocky parts and eventually get you to your destination.

### Leverage Point 6: If It Is Not Working, Stop

There is tremendous leverage in allowing yourself to stop. Admitting that something is not working, for whatever reason, will free up a lot of mental energy and release your worries and anxieties. It does not mean abandoning your objective; it simply means looking for other ways to arrive at your destination, or reviewing whether the goal you have set is still the best one.

You're not a robot. Give yourself permission to stop doing what you find so hard to do. Often when you do this, an interesting thing happens. Just by allowing yourself this safety valve and the permission to use it, you find that you are not so stressed and anxious anymore – even when you never take any time off.

Even when something is not working because you are not putting enough effort into it, it often makes more sense to stop than to try to carry on. This is useful because after a small break, you come to realize that either you'll learn to live with things as they are, meaning no improvement, or the pressure to improve grows so intense that the second time around you have enough motivation to make the change.

However, if your plan is working, do not stop for anything unless you are truly exhausted. You will often find that keeping moving gives you more energy than stopping and resting. Don't lose the momentum you've worked so hard to build up.

### Reward Yourself

Ultimately, progress can be its own best reward. Relying solely on the end result frequently leads to abandoning the effort. If you are doing some sort of fitness training just because you feel you have to, it becomes a chore, something you have to do just to get the desired end result. In doing so, you are missing a big part of the reward from this activity – the fun derived from the training itself. In order to make a lasting change, you need to derive satisfaction from the actions themselves, not just from the end result. However, while development itself has its own reward, you do need to reward yourself in other ways, too, especially at the beginning.

Delayed gratification (waiting for a future reward) is fine when you have already gathered momentum, but it can make the actions seem like a chore at the beginning. After all, you are often competing against your own bad habits which have stuck with you all this time for the reason that they give you an immediate reward (i.e. eating an unhealthy diet, skipping a planned activity, slouching in front of the TV, sleeping too late, etc.)

Plan ahead and select a few not-so-faraway milestones that are a reason to reward yourself. Don't wait until the end to celebrate your success. Often things do not work out as you had planned or the outcome is a bit unexpected, but if you just say to yourself "close but no cigar," it will not reinforce your willingness to experiment and make an effort again. Instead, think about rewarding the effort itself, not just the outcome. This makes sense since effort is what you must put forth over and over again to reach your goals. You cannot always control the exact outcome, so there has to be room for surprises. Reward the effort, not only the moments of success, and it will help you to make all your self-development activities more fun.

# 15.

## Elements for Lasting Change I:
## Take Consistent Action

Practicing consistent, targeted action is the first element for making a lasting change in your life. As much as we would sometimes like to believe otherwise, not everything can be easy, nor can it be done in a short time. When you are really trying to cultivate and develop something, whether it be your career, your state of health or your relationship, it is bound to require a prolonged effort to bring about meaningful and lasting results.

You often have to become something before you can have other things. Some things, like your health or your relationships, you can never truly possess. You have to earn them and make yourself worthy of them constantly or they will disappear. In a culture where we have grown used to "instant everything," it can feel like an awful lot of hard work to make a lasting change in our lives.

But the problem is not that changing is so difficult. We

humans have accomplished incredibly difficult things. The problem is that we expect change to be easy and effortless by some miracle, so we keep looking for that miracle, instead of accepting that it involves effort and constant work on our part. After all, to put it into perspective, quitting smoking or making a total career change is not that hard compared to some of the really arduous tasks people have had to complete in the history of humankind.

When you accept that changing takes effort, it ceases to bother you. It's when you try to fight against this fact that you get frustrated. You already know what is needed to bring about the desired results, you know what you need to do, and you know that there are no hidden "secrets." All you need is consistent action. As soon as you accept this fact, you begin to move forward with speed.

## Accept Responsibility

Hold yourself accountable for the things you can influence. You are responsible for your own thoughts, actions and feelings – the very essence of why you exist as a self-directed individual. When you respond to the world around you, when you initiate action, and when you connect the cause and effect in your life, you begin to steer yourself towards what you want.

Being responsible does not mean that you need to perform well at all times, nor does it mean that you have to always know what you are doing. There are times when you fail, times when you make no progress, times when you come up against a wall, and times when you are confused. Don't hold yourself accountable for everything. Responsibility is about acknowledging what has happened, noting the reasons, and moving on – not about trying to control everything or avoiding life's surprises and discoveries.

When you take responsibility for your actions and reactions, you create an air of quiet confidence about you. You will notice that you instinctively know what brings you closer to your goals, not because you now know something you did not know before, but because you accept what you need to do on a consistent basis and understand that there are no shortcuts. You will notice that you can find motivation and desire in day-to-day activities that earlier seemed to offer you very little. You find yourself moving from a "the big rush" motivation to a more quiet confidence which means that you don't always have to be on at full speed.

Interestingly enough, when you have this confidence the big pep talks of the motivational gurus may sound a little funny or odd. Their aim is to energize those people who are lacking a bit of motivation, but since you already feel motivated without really following any "method" advocated by one particular guru, it can all feel somehow too prescribed to you. If you have noticed this kind of effect before, you probably already have the importance of responsibility well internalized and integrated in your life.

## Choose Your Commitments

We use the word commitment in a very sloppy manner. We claim to be committed to our jobs, to be committed parents, to be committed community members, committed to this and that, all at the same time. In reality, very few people are truly committed to anything. Real commitment always involves a trade-off on your part. Your limited resources – time, money and energy – will be consistently spent on the chosen activity, leaving fewer resources for other things. You cannot be committed to everything at the same time.

Choose your commitments. There is only a limited amount you can do, be and have. Trying to make a commitment to everything will only lead to frustration. Don't take it too literally when you hear the how-to books talk about being committed to excellence in everything you do. The idea is fine; don't settle for less than what you really want to be. Understand, however, that this kind of broad excellence is an ideal, something to strive for, but it is not really completely or perfectly attainable in real life.

Commitment means closing your options down. Once you are truly committed to something, you cannot change it in a snap. Whatever you commit to, you need to learn the appropriate skills, acquire knowledge, schedule events, allocate time, commit to other people, create support systems, establish habits and work consistently. Commitment is also very emotional. If you are just going through the motions, without emotions, you are not truly committed. All this takes a great deal of effort and dedication, the very reason we use the special word commitment.

Although commitment means limiting your options, it is the only way to open up new options for what really matters. Consider this example: When you decide to aim for the very top in your chosen profession, you need to put in enough hours to become excellent at what you do. It will mean less time for other activities, no matter how interesting they are to you. Once you get to the top, however, you begin to get the kinds of privileges that were unreachable earlier. If you want to stay at the top, you need to keep working at high capacity, but you are also free to decide how to organize your activities. You will be working with the best in the field, learning from other experts and handling something more challenging than just routine work. When you get really good, you get to leave a legacy behind – a lasting contribution and an example to the other practitioners in your chosen field. Few things give as much pleasure as being able to look back on your career and know that you made a difference. None of this would be possible if you had not first made a commitment to excellence.

## Make It a "Must"

There is a big difference between "I want" and "I must." It is easy to want things – you do it all the time. You may want whatever catches your attention and makes you think that it would be nice to have. You may want dozens of things during the course of a single day and forget them as easily tomorrow. But when you must have something, it is much more serious and deliberate. To be able to create a strong sense of self-motivation, we often have to make the object of our desire a "must" – something that we just cannot do without and something that constantly stays on our mind until the issue is resolved. To reach many of the things we would like to have in our life, a mere "want" is not enough, we need to turn it into a "must" that will not let up until we fulfill it.

When we want to change, for example, we know that sometimes we need to do things that will initially feel unpleasant. Since we have conditioned ourselves throughout the years to accept as a fact that we often do not get what we want and have figured out ways of dealing with this, it is natural for us to drop the self-development effort and let go of what we want. It comes easily to us. For this reason, we may need to turn what we want into an absolute must – a thing that we cannot avoid, a thing that we simply must do. Yet we are reluctant to do it. We avoid it because we feel it takes away our freedom. We want to keep up the illusion that we are free to do whatever we want (or to not do anything at all, if we so wish), so we try to have as few musts as possible. Of course the paradox is that by not turning "wants" into "musts," we rarely get any of them.

How to go about it then? We may enlist someone else to support us and ensure that we have no way out, we may associate such powerful, positive feelings to it so that we feel we "must have it," or we may associate a powerful combination of negative feelings with the status quo, thus making the change an absolute "must" in our lives. Whatever it takes, the first step is to create such a strong motivation – a must – that it will take you through to your objective. When you learn the difference between a want and a must your ability to achieve things in life will improve tremendously.

## Focus the Natural Way

You might often find it difficult to keep your mind focused for a prolonged period of time. Your feeling of frustration is by no means lessened by the fact that you have read in how-to books over and over again how one must focus in order to achieve something. Certainly focusing can generate many benefits and bring about great power – after all, focused energy is what makes a laser cut through steel. But the truth is that focusing is sometimes overrated as a solution, and very commonly misunderstood.

A common misconception is that unless you can "stay focused" all the time, you are not very disciplined and serious about reaching your goals. However, this is one instance where trying to take consistent action (i.e. focusing all the time) may be both unnecessary and unnatural.

Consider the history of humankind and think back to a situation which could have taken place 50,000 years ago. If our ancestors had been focused or overly-concentrated on one thing for a long period of time, they would have died a premature death. What happened to the caveman who focused for hours on end on the task of skinning the deer he had caught in the middle of the forest? He died! An animal or maybe some other tribe got to him. Evolution made sure that you only stayed alive by constantly surveying your environment for possible dangers. You focused on a particular activity for a very short period of time until an unknown sound or smell caught your attention and you had to find out what it was in order to survive. This is what survival instinct is all about. Let's face it, our ancestors were cavemen who would be diagnosed these days as having a serious case of attention deficit disorder – and who for that very reason survived to become our forefathers.

Focusing nonstop is like trying to work against the history of human evolution, a battle you are more than likely to lose. However, it does not matter because you do not have to focus all the time, just for a brief period at the *right* time. Most of your tasks require concentration for a relatively short time period. Then you can let your mind wander more freely again. This is much more efficient than trying hard to focus all the time.

Consider these examples. When you go through a pile of papers, you are relatively relaxed until something catches your attention and you instantly focus on it, only to drop your focus again as soon as you realize that it wasn't so important after all.

When you drive a car on the highway, you can pay attention to the things around you but as soon as you hit that scary ten lane intersection in a strange city you immediately become alert and focused. Or, when you are working towards a college degree, you only focus on your studies for maybe six to eight hours a day, and then you shift your attention elsewhere. Very few people can or need to stay focused on one task all of the time. But, in the case of studying, what matters is that you come back to the task regularly and consistently focus for brief periods of time.

The reason most people find it hard to focus is because they are working on tasks which do not matter very much to them. But when you are working according to your own agenda, for your own reasons (even when you are formally working for some-one else), the focus comes naturally. The key is not to "try harder" to focus, the key is doing what matters to you. You cannot completely eliminate all the uninteresting tasks, but you can surely find ways to increase the amount of time you spend doing what you really love to do.

When you think about focusing or concentrating, the mental picture you have in your mind should not be of someone who looks very intense or serious, the mental effort of concentration visible in their eyes and furrowed brow. This is trying way too hard. Instead, simply enjoy what you do and you'll discover that feeling of losing yourself in whatever you do, shutting out the outside world and becoming completely at ease. You will not only get great results this way, you will also notice that you feel energized rather than drained by the activity. Call on your mental resources when they are needed, even force yourself to focus for a moment, but do not become too rigid trying to focus all day long; instead, focus dozens of times for brief moments.

## Understand The Importance of Timing

Not all time is equal. Time can be both your ally and your enemy. Some things will only work when given enough time and consistent attention. Conversely, some things will only work with a great sense of urgency. You want results fast, but you also need to realize that sometimes getting results slowly is wiser than getting them in a hurry. If you try to work against time, you will grow frustrated and impatient. When you work with time on your side, accumulating your successes, it will give you confidence knowing that eventually you will get to your destination.

Your time is your most precious resource. Use the principles outlined below to understand how time affects your personal development. Also find a good time management/life management resource to learn more about this important subject.

### Find a Balance Between Fast...

*Create a sense of urgency when necessary.* Sometimes you need to take action fast. If you delay, your intent diminishes and your mind becomes occupied with other issues. Don't postpone improving your life. Do it now. A sense of urgency is a great motivator and an energy source for a positive change.

*Seize the moment.* Don't give in to the excuse of not having enough time to spend on self-improvement. Only a few moments per day are the ones that really make a difference, and you surely have time for those. You only need a half an hour every second day to begin jogging, for example. Concentrate your energies on those few seconds when you make potentially life-changing decisions. These decisions may seem mundane to you – in this case, it is about whether you put those running shoes on and get out the door or not – but when you get this far, the rest will take care of itself. Become aware of the small defining moments and seize them.

### ...and Slow...

*Some things take their own time.* Many things have a natural rhythm that cannot be sped up; trying to do this would be futile, causing  nothing more than frustration and stress. You cannot speed up things which have their natural rhythm, no matter what you try. You cannot plant seeds and expect the crops to appear in a week. Accept that some things in personal growth only work when given enough time.

*Don't waste time by being in a hurry.* You cannot work effectively on your most important self-development tasks when you are tired or in a rush. So don't! During these unproductive hours focus on completing simple, mundane tasks that you have to get done anyway, such as organizing your papers or unloading the dishwasher. Know the difference between your most productive time of the day or night and your less productive times.

*Do things one step at a time.* You can make instant changes to your attitude, feelings and motivation, but to translate those changes into concrete results will take consistent action. You need to build a foundation first, and then acquire the skills and habits that will eventually take you to your goal. Realize that you have to pace yourself when it is going to be a long-distance trip instead of a quick spurt. This is all, however, part of the fun when you are doing what you really love to do. It is not only the destination but also the journey that matters.

### ...to Accumulate the Results

*Success is accumulated.* Lasting results rarely happen overnight. They are accumulated from a series of small, consistent improvements and combined with the interplay of little achievements and failures which have shown you what works for you. Some things are only possible when they are the result of cumulative actions – your level of fitness is a prime example. Success is accumulated because no matter how perfect the step-by-step plan or how great the advice, you need to apply it to your situation and make it your own – a process that is likely to take a while to go through.

## Take a Daily Dose of Action and a Weekly Dose of Reflection

Whenever you are in doubt or whenever you feel that your efforts are stagnating, take action. It may not solve the problem right away, but it will energize you and produce new ideas and feedback that will help you move ahead.

Take a used medicine bottle and replace the old label with a new one which proclaims in bold letters "ACTION – to be taken daily." Place the bottle on your table to remind yourself that the cure to any problem is to take some action. Use it daily in large doses and your life will take a fast turn for the better. Do the same with another bottle and label this one "REFLECTION – to be taken weekly." Use it to remind yourself to pause and reflect upon what you are doing, where you are going and what you value in life.

# 16.

# Elements for Lasting Change II: Create Habits

Turning consistent action into habits is the second element for making a lasting change in your life. Because in the end, what you are able to do (your skills) does not matter nearly as much as what you *will* do.

Ironically, when motivational speakers say that you can do absolutely anything and that there are no limits to what you can have, they may actually be hindering your success. Why? Because these claims can make you feel too good about yourself. Consider a typical motivational seminar. The presentation is very convincing, the stories about human courage touch your heart and the particular method promoted by the speaker really sounds foolproof. The problem is that it is very tempting to just mentally pat yourself on the back. When the speaker then says that you need to *take action* to realize your potential, your mind has already drifted off. At most, you make a note to begin the work sometime later, when it is more convenient for you. After all, you rationalize, you came to this seminar to gather information – the action can come next week.

How can you then make sure that you take the right action on a regular basis? The answer lies in creating habits. This skill is universal and applies across all disciplines, and it will probably do more for you than any other single thing that you learn from this book. Perhaps surprisingly, love has a lot to do with it.

### The Master Skill of Creating Habits

Learning *skills* and learning (or unlearning) *habits* are two different things that require different actions. Unfortunately, some how-to authors do not make a clear distinction between the two, leading to a lot of confusion. The easy way to understand the difference is this:

- Skills are your *ability to do something*. You have the skill to speak convincingly in front of a large audience, for example.
- Habits are what you *do constantly*. For example, speaking in front of large audiences regularly (whether you are good at it doesn't matter).

The key difference is that while skills are important, habits ultimately hold all the power over your destiny. You become what you consistently do. In getting somewhere in your life, it does not matter at all what you are able to do (skills) if you don't do it regularly (habits). Not only that, without good habits, skills are very hard to develop.

Habits are more fragile than skills. Once you develop a skill, it is likely to stay with you for a while even when you no longer practice it actively and regularly. But when you abandon one of your habits, it disappears immediately and often requires considerable effort to reestablish it in your lifestyle.

The master skill of self-improvement is creating habits because your habits define the value of what you accumulate in your life, whether it be in your career, your relationships or in any other area of your life. Habits also define who you are as a person, since you are, ultimately, your habits. If you have the habit in your life of doing loving things for others, then you are a loving person. If you have made it your habit to live a healthy lifestyle, then you are healthy. If your habit is to seek and share wisdom, then you are wise. Or if your habit is to overeat, then you are probably overweight. Whatever do you on a consistent basis is what you start to become.

Habits are powerful because they are very automatic actions, deeply ingrained in your self-identity. Habits are what you hold yourself to be as a person. They are your identity, whether you like it or not. Those people who are in the habit of crashing in front of the TV after they come home from work have succumbed to the "couch potato habit." This habit may be so ingrained in their lifestyle that even their physiology may have come to depend on it. For example, if they try to sit somewhere else in their house, they feel somehow uncomfortable, even if their position is physiologically better than it would be on the couch. They have learned to associate relaxing after work with the couch. So when they feel that they are somehow drawn towards the couch and their remote control, they are actually being drawn towards themselves; that is, they are being drawn towards what they are, their identity. They truly *are* the "after-work-couch-and-remote-control-person."

Habits, including bad ones, are deeply ingrained because they embody who you are. Your mind will do its utmost to maintain your concept of self-identity coherent and intact, making it hard to "unlearn" or discard bad habits. This is positive and useful when you have developed good habits, making it easy to keep them up in your life. Living with them is easy and changing them is hard. But when your habits are destructive it is difficult because unlearning them can take a lot of effort.

To get what you want out of life, to reach your goals, you need to create habits that pull you in the right direction and avoid the habits that pull you away from your target. Creating the right kind of habits can be difficult if you do it out of a sense of duty, for example, grimly trying to force yourself to do something. Getting rid of old habits may be even harder, because even when you know that they are not good for you, they are so deeply ingrained that the slightest slip will put you back in their grip. Luckily, there is a solution. It all becomes easy when you do it because it is something that you truly love to do.

## Creating Habits for a Lasting Change

How often have you tried something new, just to find out that you could not keep up this new habit for longer than a few days or perhaps a week? Probably more often than you care to remember! Almost all the self-help and how-to books will tell you that you must create habits and practice them constantly. And you *do* begin full of good intentions, trying to stick to your habits, but you somehow fail after a couple of weeks. By then, you conclude that this technique wasn't really suitable for you and forget the whole thing, or go searching for a new book with a new set of solutions.

The trouble is that in order to form a habit, it is necessary to practice it constantly, but many how-to books fall short of explaining exactly how this should be done. They say that you need to identify what you want, create reasons for wanting it badly enough, then resolve to get it, then take action and never give up. But this is essentially *what-to* advice, not *how-to* advice. You already know all this; what you are after is something that helps you to stick to what you are doing. Is there anything that can really ensure that you stick to your new habits and don't slip back into your old ways? Yes, there is. Together with proper goal setting, what really works is the combination of these four strategies:

- Do what you love
- Externalize
- Compound habits
- Park yourself facing downhill

### Do What You Love

You cannot achieve your biggest goals without love. Loving what you do is the answer, and there is a reason for this.

Creating habits, by definition, means creating repetition. But repeating things again and again sounds tedious and boring – unless you are doing what you love.

When you do what you love you will learn to like the repetition and find pleasure in each step that is taking you towards your goal. Taking action is easy – in fact, you can hardly wait for the new day to begin so that you can get going again. There is a purpose to what you are doing, and when the going occasionally gets tough, you know why you are doing it. You are motivated to spend the necessary time and to make an effort to learn in the true sense of the word.

This is why doing what you love is so very important. The habits come easily and you have strong reasons for sticking to them even when obstacles arise along the way. When you do what you love, you learn to enjoy the repetition of your habits the way you enjoy and look forward to eating your favorite foods over and over again.

Find out what you love to do and stay true to those things. It will make reaching those goals possible, but more than that, it will allow you to enjoy the whole process. You will begin to view your self-development efforts as a journey that you are happy to take, instead of as an unavoidable chore standing between you and your desires.

What if you have set yourself goals that you don't feel connection to? Then it is time to ask yourself why you are pursuing this particular goal in the first place. Is it something that you have to do, perhaps in payment for eventually doing something that you really love to do? If this is the case, then you know why you are doing it. If someone else has obliged you, or you want it because it has somehow become the fashion, then it is time to examine the overall direction of your life. Enroll in a course or find a self-help book that will help you determine what it is that you really want and why you want it.

We all love something. It does not have to be movie-like love with burning passion or anything on a grand scale. It can be your family, career, pet, hobby or good friend. What matters is that you have found something special that you care about. You will be motivated to do more out of love than for any other reason.

### Externalize

Seek outside help. This is perhaps the most important factor in defining whether you succeed at sticking to your new habits or whether you give up on them. Very few people have enough self-discipline to carry on day after day without any outside support. Nor should they, because we are a species that lives in societies for a very good reason: it is much more effective to do things together than alone.

Although you embody your habits and initiate new ones in your life (otherwise they are just forced actions), you should not rely solely on yourself to try to develop them. "Externalize" your new habits. Put them out of your mind and into the minds of others and into other mediums. Make them visible and tangible by writing them on your calendar, sticking a note on your refrigerator, creating a checklist, recording a message on your own answering machine, or best of all, getting someone else to give you a reminder. What is going to be more effective, just going jogging by yourself, or scheduling it on your calendar, getting your colleagues at work to ask you how your jogging is going and finding a jogging buddy who will drag you out the door no matter how much you protest?

You cannot hold too many things in your conscious mind all at the same time. It is not easy to keep a perfect checklist in your mind at every moment which reminds you to keep up your habits and which also keeps track of what you have or have not done. Your consciousness has a natural tendency to wander, and only the external help you've enlisted will help keep you on track. When you develop a habit, you need to be sure that when your mind begins to wander that your externalizations will keep reminding you to get back to the task at hand. Definitely enlist the help of other people. When you try to do it all by yourself, your mind starts to play tricks on you, you lose faith, and there is nobody to tell you that you are beginning make up excuses instead of taking action.

One reason most of us work for a firm or a public organization is the effectively externalized behavior – a system of social pressure, rules and checks and balances to make sure that we go to work every morning and stay at our desks until the afternoon. We may not always feel like going to work, but our "externalizations" get us back on the right track. Organizations help us to get things done because the environment and the situation carries us forward (read: someone comes to kick your behind when you don't show up!) This is the same reason personal fitness trainers are becoming popular and athletes have always used coaches. They push us forward when we ourselves are ready to take a day off.

There is another reason not to keep all these ideas in your head. As wonderful as your brain is, mental models can be messy, incomplete and contradictory. We need externalizations not just to serve as reminders, but also to store information, organize it, work with it, collect it, distribute it, compare it, and to make sense of it all. Put your thoughts on paper, make a list of your goals, write down your values, create a checklist of the actions you are going to take – externalize to get a better perspective of your thinking and to unclutter your mind. These externalizations can become the language you use to talk to yourself about your dreams, aspirations and goals.

Of course you do not want to become reliant on outside sources for getting things done. But going at it totally alone is not a smart choice either. Support your habits by using external resources to keep you on the right track. Use externalized information (to create lists, priorities, calendar, diary, notes, etc.) and externalized behavioral triggers (reminders, alerts, other people, etc.) to block out the "noise" that you have in your daily life. The constant demands on our attention make it difficult to keep an eye on the long-term perspective. Don't rely on your good intentions alone, externalize your habits.

### Compound Habits

Compounding habits means combining a number of habits that support each other. When you are in the habit of eating a healthy diet (which gives you energy), sticking to your decisions (which gives you self-discipline) and involving your friends in your activities (which provides you with support), creating the habit of fitness in your life is a breeze. On the other hand, if your habits include working very long hours (limiting your time and energy), trying many things but not really sticking to any of them (low self-discipline) and going about everything alone (no support from other people), no wonder you find it hard to create a habit of fitness in your life.

There are a three habits you should consider integrating into your lifestyle because they will carry you all through your life, making other habits easier to learn and maintain. These are:

- The habit of taking action
- The habit of relaxed self-discipline
- The habit of asking why and what

*Action* is what makes things happen. Even when an activity is purely intellectual, you need to take action to begin it, keep it up and then translate the results into something concrete – not to mention communicate the results to other people. Get into the action habit and your life will take a turn for the better. Don't put this off. There *is* knowledge that you need to have beforehand, but it is usually less than you think. Do your planning as you go along. This not only creates new knowledge but it also creates tremendous energy. If you tend to stay still, inertia tends to keep you where you are. If you tend to take action, it is easy to keep moving forward.

You need *self-discipline* to achieve meaningful things in your life because they always require a concentrated effort over a long period of time. There is no need to be grim and grit your teeth in an attempt to "discipline" yourself – relax a little. Discipline is not a problem when you are doing what you love. You will still have good days and bad days, but it does not feel like a chore anymore. The ability to consistently work towards your goals, even when you do not always feel like it, will get you further in life than perhaps any other thing you can learn. And luckily, when you are doing what you love, you usually feel even more motivated because the action itself brings pleasure.

Learn the habit of pausing for a moment and *asking why and what*. Ask good questions and you will get good answers. Why is this happening? Why is this important? What can I do to improve the situation? Try to make sense out of the what is happening in your life and it will be easier to take the right kind of action and easier to see the value of self-discipline.

### Park Yourself Facing Downhill

Your habits take place in time, usually activated for a short period of time (going jogging, for example), followed by a longer period of rest, inactivity or some other activities. You usually do not think about your habits, they are just part of your life and you move on to other activities when you are finished. To be effective in making new habits stick, however, you need to pay specific attention to how you begin and end your habits (activities). The trick is to do it as if you were parking your car facing downhill – if you have trouble starting the motor, the downward slope will help you get going.

Here is how: You must allocate time, by using a calendar and a pen, to the new habit that you are trying to incorportate into your lifestyle. Then you have to make a mental resolution to devote time to the activities which involve this new habit. It is best if you can also externalize this resolution so that something or someone reminds you to take proper action. Simple enough, you say.

Now comes the tricky part. Your success hinges on a number of factors that must be present. When you park yourself facing downhill, the length of the time you set for your activities must be exactly right. The time should not be too little or too much, but just right. Choose the time in a such way that it is long enough for you to get started, but short enough so that once the time is up, you actually feel like there is still something left to do. The trick is not to continue this task longer than the specified time, but to leave some work unfinished and use the last few minutes to prepare for the next time (the next day, for example) so that you can get a running start right where you left off. You should also not feel exhausted by your new activity, be it mental or physical, or it is likely that you'll gradually slip back into your old habits. If the time is too short, you'll have no time to properly do what you set out to do, and the whole exercise will seem useless or stupid. If the time you set is appropriate, you should feel a bit frustrated that this time you have allotted has come to an end and you have to wait a while to go through the exercise again. It is absolutely essential that you do not extend the time you spend on an activity after the time is up. In this case, a short-term gain in productivity is likely to destroy the long-term potential.

So in practice, if you are trying to establish the habit of making telephone sales calls, for example, you make your calls at the designated time, but before coming to the end of your list, leave one or two friendly customers for the next time. The next time you call, you begin by calling the friendly customers to help you get your momentum going instead of dreading the whole idea of getting started. If you are a writer, stop mid-paragraph, knowing what you are going to say next, and then begin with that during the next session in order to avoid writer's block. If you need to go jogging, schedule a time for a friend to come to pick you up at your front door for the next run.

This also works if your planned activity is very mentally or physically exhausting. When you know it is likely that you will have to take a small break at some point, take the break well before you have to. Leave some energy to get started after your break and this will also help you to keep your sense of control. Park yourself facing downhill and you will always have an easier time getting started and keeping those habits consistent.

## Act Like a Pro – Get Back to Basics

Isn't it odd how in professional sports at the end of the season the winning team invariably says that what made them strong was focusing on getting the basics right? The coaches never talk about discovering new tricks that nobody had been aware of before! They always exclaim that the team just worked on getting back to basics.

The more advanced you are, the more you'll understand the importance of strong basics. Basic skills and habits provide a strong and solid foundation upon which advanced skills are refined. If you have a solid foundation you will be able to better handle life's diverse and numerous circumstances than if you have just dedicated yourself to becoming competent in one particular area. You have probably already become familiar with a great deal of the available how-to and self-help ideas, but that does not make them any less relevant to your life. Bear in mind that it is not only about having the basics down that makes the difference, it is more important to put them into practice in everyday life. Working hard on the basics is what sucessfully gets the team through the season. Working hard on the basics is what will successfully get you through life.

# 17

# Elements for Lasting Change III: Expand Your Capacity

The third element for lasting change is to expand your mental and physical capacity. Once you have acquired an ability or skill and have then made it part of your identity by turning it into a habit, the next step is to grow your capacity. This is similar to increasing the power of the processor in your computer – suddenly it has the resources to do much more and getting better results becomes progressively faster. When you increase your capacity, instead of being able to run five miles, you can now run ten. Whereas you were previously exhausted after five miles, now it is easy because you have increased your maximum capacity.

When your capacity expands, you are willing and able to do things that previously would have taken a tremendous effort to accomplish. Now it comes relatively easily and you no longer have the feeling that you are forcing things to happen or that you are pushing yourself to the very limit of your powers. Always working at the upper limit of your capacity is not efficient or fun. It will require tremendous amounts of energy and willpower, leaving no reserves if something unexpected happens. The first step to expanding your capacity is to build some mental muscle.

## Train the Muscles of the Mind

Instead of wishing that everything were easy, you need to build some mental muscle. Just as your body needs conditioning if it is to function consistently at a high level of performance, so does your mind. It helps to think of your mind as a muscle. If you have not done any bodybuilding, your muscles can only lift a certain amount of weight. Setting a goal such as becoming the richest person on Earth, in addition to not being realistic or wise, is like trying to lift 1,000 pounds with untrained muscles. You will not be able to move the weight an inch and you'll just end up injuring yourself.

You need to build a foundation that supports your efforts. Luckily, the mind is so flexible that it can grow both faster and stronger than your physical muscles ever will. Many of the same principles apply to training both muscles and the mind: know your limits, train regularly, learn the proper technique and get enough rest between workouts. With some practice, it is easy to condition your mind to the level where you will simply be amazed at the results you achieve.

When you get excited about self-help advice you may try to bite off more than you can chew at first – especially if you are embarking on an activity which requires a disciplined effort seven days a week, for example. The muscles of your mind are just not up to it unless they have already been regularly trained and are in practice. They will give up and you will say to yourself, "I knew it wouldn't work because I have no self-discipline." But it is not that you lack self-discipline, you just were not prepared for this task yet. Because your self-discipline is like a muscle, a surefire way to fail a personal development program is to depend on self-discipline alone. Every time you see yourself slipping or feel your willpower faltering, you'll become frustrated and start to needlessly blame yourself. The simple solution is to create support mechanisms that will keep you going (people are the most important, for example), and little by little you'll develop that "muscle," whether it be self-discipline or something else. If you overload the muscle too much, it will not have the chance to get any stronger and it will just break down.

How do you train the "discipline muscle," for example? The answer is that you have to do things you don't want to do, but which somehow bring you closer to your goals. Those who have children know that there are certain things you simply *have to* do, whether you want to or not. Somebody has to change the diapers, for example. Parents will do it because they love their children and this is just something that needs to be done. It's no big deal – that's just how it is. Everybody can manage to do things they really do not want to do. Everybody can build some muscle when they see that it brings them closer to what they love.

## Use the Power of Compounding

If you're thinking that all this sounds like an awful lot of boring work, the truth is quite the opposite. The point is not to do just one thing day in, day out, but to develop all your skills and abilities with a bigger, more consistent purpose in mind. Staying within just one area of development, if that alone did not bore you to death, would make you a victim of the law of diminishing returns. The further you tried to go, the fewer benefits you would get in return for your efforts. The solution is to learn to compound the elements that will move you towards the things you want.

Compounding means stacking things on top of each other to achieve a greater effect. When you compound, the things on the bottom form a platform for the next things, making learning them easier and faster. By compounding skills and habits, you will get to the next level in your personal development because your whole life is enriched by the skills and habits that support each other. Your relationship will get better not only by concentrating on it alone, but also by developing communication skills, understanding your motivation and finding a balance with the other aspects of your life. Often compounding will mean less work and better results than focusing on one aspect only.

We can see the power of compounding in sports where training just one skill or one muscle group will only get you so far. Virtually every top athletic performance is based on the effect of compounding. Tiger Woods doesn't just hit golf balls. He exercises his muscles, follows a special diet, and spends hours anlyzing the game. In addition, he has to work on his mental stamina, do stretching to increase his range of movement, and test equipment. He also practices relaxation techniques and works with a whole team of people who help him to manage his training. In other words, he compounds the elements he needs for success.

Pete Sampras, the best tennis player of the 90s, started his athletic training with ballet. What does ballet have to do with tennis? As it turns out, absolutely everything! Ballet teaches balance, explosive yet resilient movement, concentration, the importance of good technique, body composure, muscle control, precision – the list goes on and on. No wonder Sampras became the number one tennis player in record time. The ballet training, as unconventional as it sounds, was an important part of compounding the elements he needed for a superb performance.

Rarely, if ever, does top performance result from any one single skill. You need to combine and compound skills and habits to achieve the life you want. Compounding also frees you from following any rigid plan to get where you want to go. You can find a combination that works for you and often you will discover that you'll reap the benefits from your compound skills in quite unexpected situations.

## Compounding Gives You More Strategies

Another way to understand the power of compounding is to think that there are two ways to increase capacity: specific and generic. If you want to have more capacity to run, train yourself by running more often. Simple enough. Direct practice like this is the specific way to increase capacity.

However, most of the things in the area of human development benefit not only from direct practice, but also from expanding your capacity in the generic sense. If you were to increase your self-discipline, for example, you would benefit from getting better at understanding your beliefs, working with your feelings, learning the proper goal setting techniques and creating motivation. All these aspects would support you in growing the capacity for self-discipline. When your self-discipline is about to fail you and you reach for that cookie jar, for example, you would remember why you think cookies are bad for you (beliefs), why you feel you need them (feelings), why those cookies won't help you reach your goal (goal setting) and how to motivate yourself not to go ahead and eat them (motivation). When you compound the effects like this it is as if you had a group of supporting muscles in your body, letting the primary muscle – in this case, the self-discipline – do its task more effectively.

Using the generic approach to expand your capacity, you begin to see many alternative strategies of reaching your goals. When you are not so dependent on specific strategies (for example, only using self-discipline to get things done), you will feel like you are living your life instead of following a ten-step plan designed by someone else. With limited capacity you tend to apply just one strategy, whether it is effective or not. You may not even dare to try the alternatives that might be more effective because this would take you into an uncharted territory and away from the strategies you have learned to use. But when your capacity grows in the generic sense, you are more flexible in getting to your destination and less exhausted after the effort. In a sense, you have a whole toolbox instead of just a hammer.

With broad capacity, you will also be more effective even when you are tired or not really focusing on the task at hand. Your mind will contain a combination of interconnected capabilities that will guide you in the right direction, even when you are not paying full attention to the task. If you always have to switch to a very narrow and specific "how-to-reach-my-goals-in-ten-steps" program in your brain, you need to pay tremendous amounts of attention to what you are doing in order not to deviate from that strict program. The danger is that any unexpected event can throw it off course.

Because the generic development of your capacity will bring you so many benefits, self-development tends to become an issue for your whole life, not something that you can compartmentalize only to your career, for example. Instead of becoming better and better at hammering, you become better at using the whole toolbox. Because you have more potential combinations to apply, more possibilities to choose from, you will see your whole life enriched in ways you've never thought possible.

## The S-Curve Revisited: Why Compounding Is the Key to Fast Progress

The power of compounding is a simple way to speed up the development in any area of your life. Remember how in Chapter 8 the S-Curve was used to explain why improvement is usually slow at first? When you compound skills and habits, you will find yourself accelerating through the S-curve faster than you ever thought possible.

By compounding skills and habits, you can stay away from the part of the S-curve where diminishing returns begin. Instead of focusing on one skill, or one habit, learn those that support each other. Do not spend all your time with books on sales to become a successful salesperson, spend time on communication skills, self-motivation skills, business strategy, fitness and time management as well. These skills all focus on and complement sales. Buying that tenth book on sales is no longer very productive, so buy something else – you will see much better results.

Compounding also speeds up the hardest part of the S-curve – getting started. If you happen to be a tennis player, you will find it very easy to learn squash or badminton. Although the game is different, they all require the same type of hand-eye coordination, racquet control, the necessary skills to read the opponent, quick movement and the ability to mentally calculate the trajectory of the ball. The more you learn, the easier it becomes to learn even more.

## How to Create Your Own Breakthroughs

Breakthroughs are possible. You are not limited to slow, incremental development towards your goals. It is not just marketing hype that tries to prove that people have improved their lives tremendously in an amazingly short time – there really are cases where this happens. Apparent "miracles" in self-help are possible for three reasons: Some areas may create a "bottleneck" impeding the rest of your development, and removing these obstructions brings fast results; sometimes hard work is getting you nowhere because you are lacking the right strategies; and sometimes just one final piece of the puzzle is missing and finding this important piece will make it all come together. Of course, several of these reasons can affect you at the same time.

### Remove the bottleneck

Most people have a few "bottlenecks" that are holding them back from realizing a great deal of their potential. Identifying and removing these bottlenecks will quickly unleash development in many areas simultaneously. These bottlenecks may be beliefs which are limiting or restricting your progress, they may be ineffective learning strategies or insufficient communication skills. Whatever they are, improvement in these areas will allow you to quickly rise to a completely new level. If a self-help seminar or a how-to book helps you to discover what is limiting you and then offers a way to overcome these obstacles, it is likely that you will see a remarkable improvement in a short time.

## Leverage the 80/20 principle

The power of the 80/20 principle is one of the reasons why self-help programs create major improvements with relatively little effort. Concentrating the effort on the key areas – improving the 20% of the things that bring 80% of the results (or removing the 20% of the "bottlenecks" that restrict 80% of your performance) – can really bring about substantial progress in a short time. Often the "cost" of an activity is not much greater for an activity that results in big rewards than for an activity that results in small rewards – no matter how hard you work, if you work on the wrong things or the things that only have very little impact on your life, you will not succeed. But once you have discovered the most appropriate strategy, getting results seems easy even in areas where all the previous hard work has brought you nothing. In addition, it is usually possible to find areas which you have previously neglected in your personal development. Hitting those with the best strategy can literally work miracles.

## Find the final piece of the puzzle

Sometimes you don't need to do anything complicated or overly difficult to get what you want. Maybe you were lacking just one final piece of the puzzle. Once you knew where to look, the problem was solved. If you have ever read a how-to book that contained superb insights which could be applied to your situation, you probably said to yourself, "I wish I had known that five years ago!" Sometimes you just need the right answer and everything else will automatically fall into place, making the problem or issue vanish as if it had never been there in the first place. This happens for example when a salesperson learns that no matter what the product or the service in question is, customers are always buying solutions and benefits, nothing else. The difficulties he or she once encountered will all but disappear when the sales approach is modified to reflect this idea and everything suddenly begins to make sense. It will not make every sales call a success, but it improves the odds tremendously.

Breakthroughs don't happen by themselves. To set them in motion, you need strong motivation followed by decisive action. We are often blind to the things we most need to develop, so you will also benefit from the help of an outside coach who can pinpoint what can be done and what the best way to go about it would be.

Couldn't you just concentrate on making the breakthroughs and forget about everything else where the progress is slower, then? Unfortunately not. Making a breakthrough can be very efficient but there is only so much low-hanging fruit to be picked. Sooner or later you will have to deal with incremental development again. It takes time but it has its benefits. For example, this type of development is steady and progress can often be broken down into steps which provide you with a sense of improvement. You get a steady flow of experiences confirming that you are moving towards your goal. If you fail to take one step, it is not such a big deal. You can soon try again, the disappointment is not so great as you already have a series of small successes behind you to boost your confidence. It may be a smart move to speed up development by looking for "speedy" breakthroughs, but also realize that a "slow" miracle is nonetheless still a miracle.

# 18.

# Elements for Lasting Change IV: Become Something

As the fourth and final element for achieving a lasting change in your life, you need to become somebody. Human experience is much more than goals and actions because life is not just about getting things, but even more about becoming something as a person. You can take action until you are blue in the face, and you can religiously practice good habits, but self-improvement will always be a chore and a forced effort unless you learn to "become" what you want.

When you want long-term happiness, material goals cannot be your only mission in life. Acquiring all those things will never make you completely happy because you also want to experience certain feelings in your lifetime; love, for example, and the only way to experience this is to become something. You cannot "have" reciprocal love before you have become something (for example, a loving person) yourself. To make a lasting change possible in your life, that change has to affect who you are as a person. It does not mean discarding the old – although sometimes that can be necessary, too – but rather becoming something more than you used to be.

Have a wider perspective on your life. Rather than being exclusively goal-driven, life should also be purpose-driven – why do you exist and what do you want to be? Goals then become ways of realizing that purpose and attaching a deadline and a definition to the actions you are taking.

### Becoming Something

Think about artists. When do artists actually start becoming artists? Is it at the moment that they create their first work? Is it at the moment that their parents first recognized their talent? Or at the moment they themselves decided that this is what they want to do and started doing it on a consistent basis?

Becoming something is about doing something consistently in your thoughts and actions. Remember how the basic principle of effective goal setting is to focus on taking the right steps instead of focusing on the outcome – imagining yourself taking those steps confidently and successfully. Why is this so important? The reason is because you are doing this not just because it will make the goal come true, but because these steps, the *becoming*, is the very goal itself.

To stay in good shape, for example, you have to adopt a lifestyle which encompasses fitness. You cannot "own" fitness in any other way. And since you have to exercise every day, you need to understand that the point is to enjoy the process itself, otherwise those fitness sessions will always feel like a chore.

Many people are unhappy because they are always trying to reach some end result, telling themselves that they will be happy when they finally reach their objective. But the most important things are not about getting something and then possessing it for the rest of our lives, but rather about becoming and being something. If you always shift your mind away from the action, imagining some far away end results, you will never be happy doing what you do and being what you are.

You can own material things, but you have to *become* in order to get what really matters in life: relationships, friends, love. This is very liberating for two reasons: First, you already have what it takes to get the really important things out of life. All it takes is your consistent action and commitment; you need very few other resources. Second, you can enjoy every moment of your life because you are free from the illusion that only results, and not the process itself, will bring happiness. When you understand this, it is easier to set the right priorities in your life and to avoid a lot of frustration – you know how to be happy right now, not just some day in the future.

What about the unpleasant tasks? Are there things that you must do in order to reach your goals that you cannot bring yourself to like – no matter how positively or constructively you think about them? Sure, these things do exist; there is no way around them. Just do them and try to keep your opinions about them on a neutral level, neither negative nor positive. When you have committed yourself to jogging year round, will you ever grow to like those cold winter mornings? Probably not. Just condition yourself to accept them and get out there and jog anyway!

## The Deepest Learning Is When You Embody
## What You Have Learned

True success comes not when you are *able to*, but rather when you *are*. You are able to do the most amazing things when you put your conscious mind to it, but you are able to do even more, more consistently, more effortlessly, when you embody what you have learned and have made it part of your identity.

This holds enormous power. It comes from unconscious activity as well as conscious. It's the power of your autopilot making the right choices – you no longer have to struggle to do something because it all comes naturally. You don't have to make a specific decision to go jogging in the mornings every day when you have become a runner – you do it automatically because that is who you are. You no longer have to think about how to behave as the manager of a company when you have internalized your role as a leader. It still may not always be easy, but when you know that this is who you are, you will have confidence in your ability to deal with these things.

The power of being something is the power of the habits you have created. When you are in shape, you have learned and internalized fitness habits. Someone may have more knowledge about fitness than you have, but unless they *are* in good shape, they aren't experiencing any of the benefits. Either you are physically fit or you aren't. It is not a possession that you can hold onto forever once you have ticked it off from your list of goals. You have to embody it all the time.

Physical fitness is an easy example to understand, but in many other areas we are not able to make these distinctions so easily until we have changed our definition of learning. Remember, it is not about knowledge. You would not say that you have learned to be physically fit if you were really out-of-shape. Similarly, it would not be truthful to claim that you are a top salesperson after you've clinched your first big deal. But when you have started to make these deals continuously you and everybody else would know that this is exactly what you are – a top salesperson.

What you have really learned oozes out of you. It is you – your identity – instead of being a piece of information that you have memorized. This is why we value experience so much – not because it has taken years to accumulate (it should come faster when you have the right skills), but because through your effort you have truly internalized and become what you have learned. For this reason, business school graduates are not given managerial positions when they apply for their first job. They may have acquired a great deal of knowledge at the university, but they are still far away from being business leaders.

*Being* will often surpass *being able to*. You will be seen as "genuine" and you know yourself that you are "genuine." This provides you with an enormous amount of power. It separates long-term success from the short term. There are always those people who put in a lot of effort and get a lucky break at the same time, leaving everyone to marvel at their overnight success. But if this person has not really internalized what it takes to keep this up constantly, even if they have a lot of raw talent, he or she will always achieve less in the long term than those who embody what they do. In fact, the more important a particular achievement is to you, the less the mastery of any single skill matters. Long term, it all comes down to being true to your cause and becoming what you learn along the way.

### The Only Way to Be Is to Be Actively

People become something by adopting specific actions, thoughts, gestures and feelings into their daily life. They constantly do what they are. You may be able to paint the most beautiful picture imaginable, but you are only an artist when you consistently paint. You may have recorded a big hit single years ago, but if that is all you have done, there is a good reason people nowadays call you a former pop star. The only way to be is to be *actively*.

Forget the picture-book illustration of a guru sitting atop a mountain and somehow being enlightened. At the heart of it, *being* means *doing repeatedly*. For example, you can't just somehow *be* nice, you have to *do* nice. You do nice things, and by doing them constantly you are (being) a nice person. What about being at peace with yourself? Isn't that just "being", without any actions? Not really. Unless you plan to withdraw from the world and have no contact with other people, you will eventually have to deal with life's surprises. It is dealing with these surprises in a peaceful manner that allows you to be at peace with yourself.

To be something is to create the appropriate habits and to practice them constantly. You are a loving husband when you constantly show loving actions towards your wife. And in doing this, you find the greatest enjoyment because you feel that you are true to your identity. There is a reason we don't say "I have love" but rather "I am in love." When you *are* a loving person it will show in everything you do.

Being something is the ultimate goal you can possibly have in life. Whether your goals include happiness, health or relationships with other people, you have to be something to have these elements in your life, and you have to be constantly, otherwise they will disappear. And that, of course, is the challenge of it. Losing excess weight on a diet and quitting smoking is a good start on your way to becoming healthy, but you really *are* healthy only when this becomes a permanent state of your being. This is why the quick fixes don't work, why the fast weight loss programs almost never produce permanent results, why winning the lottery will not make you a better person and why cheating is not the right way to get what you want. You have to *be* before you can *have*.

## Don't Be Afraid to Be an Amateur

Understand that you don't need to be good at everything you do to be able to create a change in your life. What matters is that you care enough about what you do. In a sense, this requires that you remain an amateur in your life. Amateur literally means "a lover," somebody who does things out of love. You will never get absolutely proficient in everything you do in life and nor should you. Richard Farson expressed this well in his book *Management of the Absurd* when he talked about good managers, but surely he meant all people as well:

> *"Amateurism is what makes managers give so much of themselves to their jobs; it's what gives them such a fondness for their jobs, even when the jobs are difficult, stressful, and frustrating."*
> – Richard Farson

Even when you're not always on top of everything, even when you are confused or tired, you do things out of love. You are not in it just for the results, you love the process itself. Whether an amateur gardener, photographer or athlete, amateurism is what gives us the pleasure in our actions, and ultimately, the most natural way to a lasting change.

# 19.

## Living a Life of Growth

Life is not a game, it is more like free-flowing, spontaneous play. It is not so much about keeping score as it is about enjoying yourself, developing your abilities, making new discoveries and connecting with other people. Self-help advice shouldn't be about trying to "win" the game of life; it should be about discovering and appreciating all the wonderful possibilities in the "play" of life.

A life is lived the best way possible when you feel that you are doing good things and getting closer to what you want to have and become. Sensing that you are moving forward and fully participating in what life has to offer provides great satisfaction.

It is easy to get confused and take all the self-improvement advice a little too seriously, such as concentrating too much on the anticipated achievements and forgetting to enjoy the process. If you have ever observed a work in progress – a good metaphor for your life – you know it is always a bit messy. There are bits and pieces lying around, there is that tool you dropped on your toes, there is noise and hustle, and there are onlookers giving advice but unwilling or unable to help with the work at hand. So it is with self-improvement, too. Your life is not a computer that can be cleanly programmed to result in perfect output, but rather a work in progress which may look a little confusing and disorganized at times until all the beauty emerges. So more power to you if you can appreciate all the messy work itself and not just the end results.

### Enjoy the Ride

We all want to reach our goals and we feel disappointed when we don't get what we want. We are not always working towards a goal for the fun of it, there are actual objectives we want to achieve. So we might get defensive when we hear the old saying that it is not always the destination but the journey that really counts. The problem is, for most of us "personal development journey" sounds too dramatic. You just wanted to quit smoking or earn more money, not find the path to divine enlightenment!

Just relax. Think about it this way: the journey is like a career. You do not embark on a career just to achieve some final outcome such as money or to become the top manager of a big company. Sure, these things are important, but you also select the career for the career itself. Because it interests you and intrigues you. Because it is something you have always wanted to do.

Being happy is the most important reason to see your life as a journey. For you to be happy most of the time, happiness must come from the journey. Working day after day just to achieve your goals and thinking that satisfaction comes from reaching them leaves you with an awful lot of time to be dissatisfied. In fact, you will be dissatisfied most of the time. Besides, there are many things that you cannot just have or possess, rather they need to be maintained instead. Your health, physical fitness, and relationships with other people are typical examples. If you stop this ongoing maintenance, they will soon disappear. When you view your self-improvement and life in general as a journey, you are free to enjoy every moment and get pleasure from both the achievements and the work itself.

When you are in it for the journey, things change. You will be working as much towards yourself as towards external goals; you will be looking at a wider area where you can apply what you learn; you will occasionally take detours to round up your understanding of the issues; and you will sometimes arrive at your destination via a route you would never have considered were it not for the unexpected things that you picked up along the way. A journey will allow you to see how things are interconnected. For example, you will no longer try to lose weight just by going on that new diet, but also by improving your daily habits, as well as your beliefs about eating, exercising and dieting. And when you are no longer just interested in losing weight, but also in becoming healthier in a more general sense, you are then embarking upon a journey.

In fact, if you don't have too many immediate goals, and just feel drawn to the breadth of what is out there in the self-help and how-to resources, your mind may be telling you that it is interested in the journey itself. If your goals are somewhat undefined, but you are really interested in how-to and self-improvement in general, you may have actually discovered one of your big goals – the journey into yourself. This may be the very reason you

picked up those self-help books in the first place. After this realization, the concrete goals will easily find their place in the big
picture.

## Find Happiness by Finding What You Love

You can decide to be happy all the time. Self-help books have
been saying it for years: feeling happy does not depend on outside events, it is something that you create and control yourself.
Feelings just don't happen to us, they are the results of our interpretation of the outside world and our reaction to it. In fact, you
don't even need any outside stimuli – happiness is a mental state
that you can produce purely at will. When you are happy, it is
because you interpret your internal world (thoughts) and external
world (outside events) in a certain way and based on this interpretation you decide to feel the way you feel. You truly decide
whether you are happy or not. (If this is news to you, you'll be
doing yourself a big favor by finding out more about happiness
from the how-to and self-help resources.)

We lose many opportunities to be happy when we think that
happiness only comes from reaching our goals, or by experiencing something unique, or when we feel smug because we are better than someone else.

So, if you *can* be happy all the time, *should* you? Of course
not. You cannot be 100% happy with absolutely everything
because if you are, your development will stop. It is also common sense that there is no reason to mask reality by being happy
with your life if it is in fact going downhill.

It is important to realize that happiness is not comprised of
just one feeling. From intellectual to physical, to emotional to
interpersonal, happiness is multifaceted. And because there are

different kinds of happiness – from feeling utter joy to being quietly confident to being a proud parent – we need different ways to express them. There is instant happiness, daily happiness and longer-term happiness. It is not important what we call them, the important thing is to recognize that there are different types of happiness and pay attention to them. A point to remember is that many people have never "trained" happiness, so they do not necessarily know how to become happier. Yet this wisdom is centuries old, expressed in the age-old, simple advice of stopping to pay attention to the beauty all around us. Happiness comes from searching for it in everyday life, something which will not happen by itself.

To find happiness, discover what you love and appreciate. Being happy can be very simple. Do what you love. Love what you do. Know how to go about this, and the rest follows. Don't just do what you are good at (although often you need or want to do that as well), do what you really love to do.

You do not need to think so much about whether your life is "in order" or "fulfilled" if you know you are acting every day to move towards what you want to be and have. Happiness comes from evolving as a human being and moving in a direction that makes sense to you. It comes from knowing that although you cannot control the individual events in life, you are in control of the direction and you know where you are going.

## Teaching Is Learning

Teaching is a higher form of learning. The way to learn more yourself is to try to teach or coach others. It will force you examine your motives and put together a coherent structure for the ideas, plan and practice. What you are able to teach others, you have really learned for yourself.

That is what keeps so many of the self-help gurus going year after year. They embody the message by teaching it to others. Yet most of us, at least initially, do not want to become teachers. We want to improve our own life first, and besides, teaching sounds too much like pushing your ideas on other people. Sometimes, however, people start spreading what they have learned and start to embody it without even realizing it. If this happens naturally, you have internalized the ideas to the point where they come through in everything you do.

Whether you teach or coach, you also need somebody to coach you. The best people in their field share a common feature – they all have or have had help from coaches or mentors at the formative stages of their careers. This does not have to mean a full-time paid coach like many athletes have; it can also be a regular meeting a couple of times a year with an expert in your field of interest.

Finding a teacher or a coach is very effective for three reasons. First, you receive feedback that is often more objective than what you could give to yourself. Second, you get the benefit of experience, helping yourself to analyze the situation and plan what you should do next. A good coach has learned things that both complement and challenge your way of thinking. He or she can take away some of the uncertainty by recognizing from their own experience what works at the different stages of your development. Third, working with somebody else will make you push yourself harder than you would if you were working alone. You will do more with and for that person than you would do by yourself.

It is a big step to become "teachable" and "coachable." You

have learned how to appreciate the value of a pair of outside eyes and that means that you are serious about getting better in your chosen field. It is also usually the only way to become the best you can be.

When you are ready to invest your time and energy in a coaching relationship, find someone with experience, objectivity and the willingness to help. If this sounds like a lot to ask, you're right – it is. People are willing to share, but always ask yourself what you can give in return. If a one-to-one relationship is not feasible, see if you can pool a number of students to make the proposition more appealing to the teacher.

The places to begin are *communities of practice*. Ranging from dog groomers associations to million dollar sales clubs, communities of practice are organizations, clubs, networks or informal gatherings of people who are interested in the same topics. They are places to find like-minded people, share your ideas, get feedback from others, hear stories, get advice and find additional resources. They can be on the Internet or they can be found in your neighborhood. Once you become aware of what you want to develop, this automatically begins to draw your attention towards people who share similar interests. Often, it is also the first step towards finding a coach who can further help you.

Communities of practice are effective because much of what you want to do involves an aspect of society. You could not achieve your goals in a vacuum even if you wanted to. From sales success to public speaking to parenting, you need feedback from other people to see if you are on the right track. You also need to test and practice with other people, reflect on their experiences, and speed up your progress from what you can learn from their experiences. Join or found a community of practice. It is not only one of the best ways to learn, but it is also fun.

## Making Meaning of Your New Life

To make meaning of the new life you are creating for yourself, examine the past, present and the future. You have probably heard over and over again that you should live in the present moment because that is what counts and it is the only thing you can influence. This is true. When you are taking action, your mind should concentrate on the present. But the human mind has the wonderful ability to both go back in time and to imagine the future. In your mind, you can relive the past and plan the future. To make meaning of your new life, pause to reflect and think about all three times: what you have done, what you are doing and what you are going to do. Find something to enjoy about all of them.

You do not only design your life and populate it with the objectives you are trying to reach – you also evolve. Sometimes your actions, other people and circumstances cause you to evolve in quite unexpected ways. Very few people would want to know everything about their future beforehand because it would take so much away from what it is to be human and what makes life interesting. Your life is your greatest do-it-yourself experiment, so by all means plan, but discover as well.

Enjoy not only your own progress, but also the progress of others. Although you can do much more than you've probably ever imagined, you cannot do everything or become everything in one lifetime. So enjoy every moment, even when you are striving for something difficult and feel like work in progress. Share your joy with others so that they in turn will share it with you, letting you touch happiness beyond yourself.

Most of all, care. There are some people who don't care much about their lives. They are just going through the motions, never really feeling joy or fulfillment, sadness or disappointment. You must care and believe in something because this is what makes life matter to you and to others. If you don't care, if there is nothing that is special to you, if it doesn't matter one way or another what happens, what is the point of it all? Care about your life, even when you feel it is incomplete. Only when you care, can you begin to make a change.

When you have learned many new skills, acquired new habits and reached a level that you would call success, it is important to have enough humility to realize that there is still a lot to learn. Measure yourself against the best *you* can be, not against other people. Keep risking failure, not because you want to live your life on the edge, but because you want to stay true to yourself and your dreams.

Very few elderly people seem to regret the chances they have taken in their lives. Instead, they always seem to regret what they didn't do in their lives. Fully participating in what life has to offer means that things will not always go as planned, but if you stay true to yourself, this doesn't matter. What matters is that you didn't just stand on the sidelines, but that you played an active role.

To get the most out of life, do what you love and love what you do. Don't limit your activities to only those that you are already good at and which bring good results. You do not have to be good at something, you do not have to know how to do it perfectly, you just have to find out what you deeply care about. You have been reading this book long enough, so get up and get going, it will give you more energy. Do not wait, do not let the intention die. Do not wait – now is a perfect time to begin!

# Acknowledgements

I would like to thank everybody who assisted me in researching and writing this book. I have enjoyed sharing ideas at every stage of this project with people too numerous to mention here – your feedback has been invaluable.

I'd especially like to thank Raigan Bastianoni-Störzer for proofreading and providing me with important feedback on the first draft of the manuscript. I appreciate the outstanding copy-editing and valuable commentary.

Boris Budeck's and Volker Fiedler's design skills also contributed greatly to the book.

Thanks as well to Pekka Lemettinen and Antti Aho for your feedback. I'd like to thank Wolfgang Bialon and Mikko Tarkkala at Rivion for believing in the project.

Thank you, Tiina, for your patience and good humor during the process.

Finally, I'd like to thank all the people who have shared their numerous life experiences, wisdom and insight by writing how-to and self-help books. It has been a great experience to learn from you.

# APPENDIX:

## Resources to Use

Literally, everything you need to know is out there. Today there is a broader range of self-help and how-to resources available than ever before. In fact, you are often flooded with choice. Especially on popular themes, there are always hundreds of books, audiotapes and workshops available. If we define the how-to/self-help/advice category broadly enough, almost all the instructional books fall into it. There are tens of thousands of them available – books with the words "How to…" in their title alone number in the thousands.

This book cannot begin to list all the available resources, it can just provide you with a few examples that will in turn lead you further in your search. The titles selected here have helped many people and should provide a good starting point. Nevertheless, some of them will be more relevant to you than others and there is no reason to agree with any single book completely. Use the power of the Internet and the databases at bookstores to find out what else is available. Check the Web site of this book at *www.howtoselfhelp.com* for an updated and expanded list. Or just spend a rainy day at your local library or bookstore – you'll be amazed at what you can find.

Remember, the perfect book is not always the number one bestseller or the valued classic, the best book is the one that gets you started today. Grab one and begin. No book can work magic, only you can.

(Note: Most self-help/how-to books are sold as paperbacks. Sometimes hardcover editions turn into revised paperback editions, special editions, reissues and other formats that can make it difficult to trace the original format or year of publication. The following list includes editions that are currently available. When searching for these books, it is best to go with the title and the author's name, and then get any edition you find.)

*General Self-Improvement / Motivational*

Albom, Mitch. *Tuesdays with Morrie: An Old Man, a Young Man, and Life's Greatest Lesson* (New York: Doubleday 1997)

Allen, James. *As A Man Thinketh* (Los Angeles: DeVorss & Co. 1983, Reissue edition)

Anderson, Walter. *The Confidence Course: Seven Steps to Self-Fulfillment* (New York: HarperPerennial 1998)

Breathnach, Sarah, *Simple Abundance: A Daybook of Comfort and Joy* (New York: Warner Books 1995)

Carnegie, Dale. and Carnegie, D. (ed.) and Pell, A. R. (ed.) *How to Win Friends and Influence People* (New York: Pocket Books 1994, Reissue edition)

Canfield, Jack. (ed.) and Hansen, Mark Victor. (ed.) *Chicken Soup for the Soul: 101 Stories to Open the Heart & Rekindle the Spirit* (Series) (Deerfield Beach: Health Communications 1995, Revised edition)

Chandler, Steve. *Reinventing Yourself: How to Become the Person You've Always Wanted to Be* (Franklin Lakes: Career Press 1998)

Chopra, Deepak. *The Seven Spiritual Laws of Success: A Practical Guide to the Fulfillment of Your Dreams* (San Rafael: Amber-Allen Publishing 1995)

Choquette, Sonia., Tully, Patric. *Your Heart's Desire: Instructions for Creating the Life You Really Want* (New York: Crown Publishing 1997)

⁕ Covey, Stephen R. *The Seven Habits of Highly Effective People: Restoring the Character Ethic* (New York: Simon & Schuster 1990)

Cutler, Howard C. and Dalai Lama. *The Art of Happiness: A Handbook for Living* (New York: Riverhead Books 1998)

Ditzler, Jinny S. *Your Best Year Yet! A Proven Method for Making the Next 12 Months your Most Successful Ever* (London: Thorsons 1994)

⁕ Dyer, Wayne, W. *Your Erroneous Zones* (New York: Harper Mass Market Paperback 1997, Reissue edition)

⁕ Hill, Napoleon. *Think and Grow Rich* (New York: Fawcett Books 1990, Reissue edition)

Jeffers, Susan. *Feel the Fear and Do It Anyway* (New York: Fawcett Books 1992, Reissue edition)

Kiev, Ari. *A Strategy for Daily Living: The Classic Guide to Success and Fulfillment* (New York: Free Press 1997, Revised edition)

Levoy, Gregg M. *Callings: Finding and Following an Authentic Life* (Three Rivers Press 1998)

• McGraw, Phillip, C. *Life Strategies: Doing What Works, Doing What Matters* (New York: Hyperion 2000)

• Peale, Norman. Vincent. *The Power of Positive Thinking* (New York: Ballantine Books 1996, Reissue edition)

• Richardson, Cheryl. *Life Makeovers* (New York: Broadway Books 2000)

Riley, Pat. *The Winner Within: A Life Plan for Team Players* (New York: Berkley Books 1993)

Robbins, Anthony. *Awaken the Giant Within: How to Take Immediate Control of Your Mental, Emotional, Physical & Financial Destiny* (New York: Fireside 1991)

Rohn, Jim. and Rohn, James, E. *7 Strategies for Wealth & Happiness: Power Ideas from America's Foremost Business Philosopher* (Roseville: Prima Publishing 1996)

Salmansohn, Karen. and Zinzell, Don. *How to Be Happy, Dammit: A Cynic's Guide to Spiritual Happiness* (Celestial Arts 2001)

• Scott, M. Peck. *The Road Less Traveled* (Series) (New York: Simon & Schuster 1997, International edition)

Schwartz, David J. *Magic of Thinking Big* (New York: Fireside 1987, Reprint edition)

Seligman, Martin P. *What You Can Change... and What You Can't: The Complete Guide to Successful Self-Improvement: Learning to Accept Who You Are* (New York: Fawcett Books 1995)

Sher, Barbara. with Smith, Barbara. *I Could Do Anything If I Only Knew What It Was* (New York: Dell Trade Paperback 1994)

Tolle, Eckhardt. *The Power of Now: A Guide to Spiritual Enlightenment* (New York: New World Library 1999)

Tracy, Brian. *Maximum Achievement: Strategies and Skills That Will Unlock Your Hidden Powers to Succeed* (New York: Fireside 1993)

Vanzant, Iyanla. *One Day My Soul Just Opened Up: 40 Days and 40 Nights Towards Spiritual Strength and Personal Growth* (New York: Fireside 1998)

Waitley, Denis. *The New Dynamics of Winning* (New York: Quill 1993)

Willis, Suzanne. *Create A Life That Tickles Your Soul: Finding Peace, Passion, & Purpose* (Doylestown: Tower Hill Press 2000)

Ziglar, Zig. *See You at the Top: 25th Anniversary Edition* (Gretna: Pelican Publishing 2000, Revised edition)

*Relationships / Family / Parenting*

⌐ Chapman, Gary. *The Five Love Languages: How to Express Heart-felt Commitment to Your Mate* (Chicago: Northfield Publishing 1992)

Gray, John. *Men Are from Mars, Women Are from Venus: A Practical Guide for Improving Communication and Getting What You Want in Your Relationships* (Series) (New York: HarperCollins 1992)

Williamson, Marianne. *A Return to Love: Reflections on the Principles of a Course in Miracles* (New York: HarperCollins 1996)

‣ Schlessinger, Laura. *Ten Stupid Things Women Do to Mess Up Their Lives* (New York: Harperperennial Library 1995)

Eisenberg, Arlene., Murkoff, Heidi E. and Hathaway, Sandee E. *What to Expect When You're Expecting* (New York: Workman Publishing Company 1996, Revised edition)

Lundberg, Gary B. and Sounders Lundberg, Joy. *I Don't Have to Make Everything All Better: Six Practical Principles That Empower Others to Solve Their Own Problems While Enriching Your Relationships* (New York: Penguin 2000)

McWilliams, Peter., Boomfield, Harold H., Colgrove, Melba. *How to Survive the Loss of a Love* (Los Angeles: Mary Books / Prelude Press 1993, Reprint edition)

Norwood, Robin. *Women Who Love Too Much: When You Keep Wishing and Hoping He'll Change* (New York: Pocket Books 1991, Reissue edition)

Pease, Allan., Pease, Barbara. *Why Men Don't Listen and Women Can't Read Maps: How We're Different and What to Do About It* (New York: Broadway Books 2001)

Phelan, Thomas W. *1-2-3 Magic: Effective Discipline for Children 2-12* (Child Management 1996, Revised edition)

### Health

Atkins Robert C. *Dr. Atkins' New Diet Revolution* (New York: Avon 1997)

Castelli, William P. and Griffin, Glen C. *Good Fat, Bad Fat: How to Lower Your Cholesterol and Reduce the Odds of a Heart Attack* (Boulder: Fisher Books, 1997)

Heller, Rachael F. and Heller Richard F. *The Carbohydrate Addict's Diet: The Lifelong Solution to Yo-Yo Dieting* (New American Library 1999, Reprint edition)

Mittleman, Stu. *Slow Burn: Burn Fat Faster by Exercising Slower* (New York: Quill 2001)

Oster, Nancy., Thomas, Lucy., Joseff, Darol., Love, Susan. *Making Informed Medical Decisions: Where to Look and How to Use What You Find* (Cambridge: O'Reilly & Associates 2000)

Phillips, Bill. and D'Orso, Michael. (contr.) *Body for Life: 12 Weeks to Mental and Physical Strength* (New York: Harper Collins 1999)

• Sears, Barry. with Lawren, Bill. (contr.) *The Zone: A Dietary Road Map to Lose Weight Permanently: Reset Your Genetic Code: Prevent Disease: Achieve Maximum Physical Performance* (New York: HarperCollins 1995)

Sobel, Dava. and Klein, Arthur C. (contr.) *Backache: What Exercises Work* (New York: St. Martin's Press 1996)

Willett, Walter C., Skerret, P. J., Giovannucci, Edward L. *Eat, Drink, and Be Healthy: The Harvard Medical School Guide to Healthy Eating* (New York: Simon & Schuster 2001)

## Wealth

Clason, George S. *The Richest Man in Babylon* (New York: New American Library 1997, Reissue edition)

Givens, Charles J. and Miller, Tom (ed.) *More Wealth Without Risk: How to Develop a Personal Fortune Without Going Out on a Limb* (New York: Pocket Books 1995, Updated edition)

Graham, Benjamin. *The Intelligent Investor: A Book of Practical Counsel* (New York: HarperCollings 1985, Revised edition)

• Kiyosaki, Robert T. and Lechter, Sharon L. *Rich Dad, Poor Dad: What the Rich Teach Their Kids About Money – That the Poor and Middle Class Do Not!* (New York: Warner Books 2000)

Lynch, Peter. and Rothchild, John. *Learn to Earn: A Beginners Guide to the Basics of Investing and Business* (New York: Fireside 1995)

Morris, Kenneth M., Morris, Virginia B., Siegel, Alan M. *The Wall Street Journal Guide to Understanding Money & Investing* (New York: Fireside 1999)

* Orman, Suze. *The Road to Wealth: A Comprehensive Guide to Your Money – Everything You Need to Know in Good and Bad Times* (New York: Riverhead Books 2001)

**Business**

Benton, D. A. *How to Think Like a CEO: The 22 Vital Traits You Need to Be the Person at the Top* (New York: Warner Books 1996)

Blanchard, Ken. *The Heart of a Leader* (Honor Books 1999)

Fischer, Roger., Ury, William., Patton Bruce. (ed.) *Getting to Yes: Negotiating an Agreement Without Giving In* (New York: Penguin USA 1991)

Girard, Joe., Brown, Stanley H. (contr.) *How to Sell Anything to Anybody* (New York: Warner Books 2001, Reprint edition)

Izzo, John B. and Withers Pam. *Values-Shift: The New Work Ethic and What it Means for Business* (Lions Bay: Fairwinds Press 2001)

Mackay, Harvey. *Swim With the Sharks Without Being Eaten Alive: Outsell, Outmanage, Outmotivate, and Outnegotiate Your Competition* (New York: Ballantine Books 1996, Reissue edition)

McCormack, Mark H. *What They Don't Teach You at Harvard Business School* (New York: Bantam Doubleday Dell 1988, Reissue edition)

Sewell, Carl. and Brown, Paul B. *Customers for Life: How to Turn That One-Time Buyer into a Lifetime Customer* (New York: Pocket Books 1998, Revised edition)

Farson, Richard. *Management of the Absurd: Paradoxes in Leadership* (New York: Touchstone/Simon & Schuster 1996)

Robbins, Harvey A. and Finley, Michael. *The New Why Teams Don't Work: What Goes Wrong and How to Make It Right* (San Francisco: Berret-Koehler 2000)

Weiss, Alan. *The Unofficial Guide to Power Managing* (Foster City: IDG Books 2000)

*Various Other Resources / How-To and Self-Help Books*

Bliss, Edwin C. *Doing It Now: A Twelve-Step Program for Curing Procrastination and Achieving Your Goals* (New York: Bantam Books 1983)

• Bolles, Richard N. *What Color is Your Parachute? A Practical Manual for Job-Hunters & Career-Changers* (Berkeley: Ten Speed Press 2002)

de Bono, Edward. *Serious Creativity: Using the Power of Lateral Thinking to Create New Ideas* (London: HarperCollins 1992)

Buzan, Tony. and Buzan Barry (contr.). *The Mind Map Book: How to Use Radiant Thinking to Maximize Your Brain's Untapped Potential* (New York: Plume 1996, Reprint edition)

Csikszentmihalyi, Mihaly. *Flow: The Psychology of Optimal Experience* (New York: HarperCollins 1991)

Fennel, Jan. *The Dog Listener: A Noted Expert Tells You How to Communicate with Your Dog for Willing Cooperation* (New York: Harper Resource 2001)

Gallwey, Timothy W. *The Inner Game of Tennis* (New York: Random House, 1997, Revised edition)

Goleman, Daniel. *Emotional Intelligence* (New York, Bantam Books 1997, Reprint edition)

Loehr, James E. *Stress for Success* (New York: Times Books 1998)

Lucas, Bill. *Power Up your Mind: Learn Faster, Work Smarter* (London: Nicholas Brealey 2001)

Meyer, Kathleen. *How to Shit in the Woods: An Environmentally Sound Approach to a Lost Art* (Berkeley: Ten Speed Press 1994)

O'Connor Joseph. and Seymor John. *Introducing Neuro-Linguistic Programming: Psychological Skills for Understanding and Influencing People* (New York: Thorsons Publishing 2000)

Oshry, Barry. *Leading Systems: Lessons from the Power Lab* (San Francisco: Berret-Koehler 1999) – Systems thinking

Senge, Peter M. *The Fifth Discipline* (New York: Doubleday Currency, 1990) – Systems thinking

Stone, Douglas., Patton, Bruce., Heen Sheila., Fisher, Roger. *Difficult Conversations: How to Discuss what Matters Most* (New York: Penguin USA 2000)

Tannen, Deborah. *You Just don't Understand: Women and Men in Conversation* (New York: Ballantine Books 1991)

Vongerichten Jean-Georges. and Bittman, Mark. *Simple to Spectacular: How to Take One Basic Recipe to Four Levels of Sophistication* (New York: Broadway Books 2000)

*Audio*

There are thousands of self-help/how-to audio programs on offer. Most of the audiotapes are based on books. Some are based on seminars and recorded with a live audience. Since many of the bestselling book titles are turned into audio versions, it does not make sense to list them here again. Instead, here is a list of sources for audio programs.

Any larger local bookstore will usually carry hundreds of audio books. In addition, there are some specialty stores which are focused on audio books only. Consult the Yellow Pages and your local business directories.

Just enter the words 'audio books' to a search engine, and you will find hundreds of companies offering audio programmes to be mail-ordered or downloaded directly. Some will let you rent tapes or CDs. Here are a few (number included if the company also takes telephone orders):

www.audioeditions.com, 800-231-4261
www.abcdinc.com, 888-749-6342
www.audible.com
www.audiobookclub.com / www.mediabay.com
www.audiobooksonline.com, 800-639-1862
www.booksontape.com, 800-626-3333
www.powells.com/psection/audiobooks.html, 866-201-7601
www.recordedbooks.com, 800-638-1304
www.talkingbookworld.com

You can also find thousands of audio books on Amazon.com and Barnesandnoble.com Web sites. Many book publishers will also offer audio books on their Web sites.

Check also the Web site of this book at: *www.howtoselfhelp.com* for additional resources and a link list to other Web sites.

About the Author: Janne Ruokonen has worked as a manager and consultant, actively putting personal development ideas to work for himself and his staff. He holds a M.Sc. degree in Management and Organizational Psychology.